World Meeting of Families 2015 and The Philadelphia Inquirer present

# POPE FRANCIS
## —— IN AMERICA ——

The Philadelphia Inquirer

WORLD
MEETING OF
FAMILIES
2015 Philadelphia

# ACKNOWLEDGMENTS

## The Philadelphia Inquirer

Published by Pediment Publishing, a division of The Pediment Group, Inc. www.pediment.com.

Printed in the United States of America.

**FRONT COVER:** Pope Francis at the at the Festival of Families on the Benjamin Franklin Parkway, Sept. 26. *Yong Kim / Staff Photographer*

**BACK COVER:** Pope Francis arrives at the Basilica of SS. Peter and Paul on Sept. 26. *Clem Murray / Staff Photographer*

**FRONT COVER FLAP:** Pope Francis addresses the Festival of Families. *Clem Murray / Staff Photographer*

**BACK COVER FLAP:** A rosary hangs from a fence on Independence Mall as the crowd waits for Pope Francis to arrive. *David Maialetti / Staff Photographer*

**OPPOSITE:** Some pilgrims left a message, others just signed their names to large posters of Pope Francis on display during the papal visit. *Elizabeth Robertson / Staff Photographer*

This book was compiled from the work of Philadelphia Inquirer and Philadelphia Daily News reporters, photographers and editors before and during Pope Francis' visit to the United States.

**Story editors:** Nancy Campbell Albritton, Michael Schaffer

**Executive Photo Editor and Design Director:** Michael Mercanti

**Assistant photo editor:** Jessica Griffin

**Contributing photo editors:** Alen Malott, Cheryl Shugars

**Photographers:** Clem Murray, David Maialetti, Yong Kim, Michael Bryant, Tom Gralish, David Swanson, Elizabeth Robertson, Alejandro A. Alvarez, Steven M. Falk, Charles Fox, Ed Hille, Matthew Hall, Joseph Kaczmarek, Bradley C. Bower, Jonathan Wilson, Wanda Thomas, Aaron Windhorst, Emily Cohen, Mary D'Anella, Mark C. Psoras, Joseph Gidjunis, Stephanie Aaronson

**Reporters:** David O'Reilly, Julia Terruso, Kristin Holmes, Claudia Vargas, Sofiya Ballin, Jonathan Tamari, Tricia Nadolny, Maria Panaritis, Michael Matza, Michael Boren, Jeff Gammage, Jacqueline L. Urgo, Kristen Graham, Aubrey Whelan, Jason Laughlin, Melanie Burney, Amy Rosenberg, Mari Schaefer, Michaelle Bond, Laura McCrystal, Rita Giordano, Mark Fazlollah, Samantha Melamed, Mike Newall, Chris Palmer, Allison Steele, Susan Snyder, Ben Finley, Diane Mastrull, Justine McDaniel, Don Sapatkin, Caitlin McCabe, Chris Brennan, David Patrick Stearns, Inga Saffron, Elizabeth Wellington, Dan DeLuca, Peter Dobrin, Joseph N. DiStefano, Kathy Boccella, Tom Avril, Angelo Fichera, Jeremy Roebuck, Craig McCoy, John Timpane, Tony Wood, Chris Hepp, Dylan Purcell, Joe Gambardello, Stephanie Farr, Regina Medina, Vinny Vella, Dan Geringer, William Bender, Mari A. Schaefer

**Managing Editors:** Sandra M. Clark, Gabriel Escobar

**Marketing:** Fred Groser, Matthew Broad, John Gilpin, Emily Schriner

**Design:** Chris Fenison

**Contributing designer:** Sterling Chen

**Special thanks:** The Philadelphia Inquirer gratefully acknowledges the kind cooperation of Archbishop Charles J. Chaput and the Archdiocese of Philadelphia and President Robert J. Ciaruffoli and Executive Director Donna Crilley Farrell of the World Meeting of Families; Kenneth A. Gavin, Director of Communications at the Archdiocese of Philadelphia; Meg Kane, Vice President, Brian Communications.

# TABLE OF CONTENTS

**OPPOSITE:** Hundreds of ciboria, the golden vessels used to hold consecrated hosts, await the distribution of Communion at Pope Francis' Mass on the Parkway. *Michael Bryant / Staff Photographer*

Dear Readers,

As Chairman of the Board of Philadelphia Media Network, I'm proud and honored that our company has partnered with the World Meeting of Families to produce this official commemorative keepsake book, *Pope Francis in America*.

When I took the helm of The Philadelphia Inquirer, Daily News and Philly.com, I said, "Every great city needs a great newspaper." The visit of Pope Francis for the World Meeting of Families was just another example of the greatness of our city. And I'm sure, as you turn the pages of this book, read the articles and look at the memorable photos, you'll agree that the Philadelphia Media Network has the talented staff to produce great content in print and online.

I hope you and your family will treasure this book in the years to come. When you page through it, I hope you'll remember the feeling of unity that swept through our city, the spirit of hospitality exercised by our residents, the fine work of our city and public safety personnel, and the magical time when the eyes of the world turned to Philadelphia for inspiration.

Finally, I'd like to thank the World Meeting of Families and our sponsors who made our publication of this book possible.

Yours truly,

*Gerry*

H. F. Lenfest
Owner & Chairman of the Board
Philadelphia Media Network

PHILADELPHIA MEDIA NETWORK

The Inquirer  DAILY NEWS  philly●com

Dear Friends,

The Archdiocese of Philadelphia and the entire Philadelphia region have just experienced a historic and momentous week. The World Meeting of Families – Philadelphia 2015 and the visit of Pope Francis were sources of great joy for the entire country. In Philadelphia – the City of Brotherly Love and Sisterly Affection – the Holy Father's appearances created irreplaceable moments in history.

We were honored to host visitors from over 100 countries who participated in the World Meeting of Families Congress. It was the largest such gathering in the history of this global event, bringing more than 20,000 people together to celebrate the importance of family and explore ways to overcome the many challenges that threaten the stability of family life.

Familial love embraces all of humanity. As such, our speakers for the Congress reflected the global diversity of belief. They included Catholics, Protestants, Latter Day Saints, Jews, and Muslims. Regardless of faith background, healthy families are the key to authentic human development worldwide: the kind of development that serves the whole human person, body and soul.

Pope Francis is one of the most popular and magnetic religious and world leaders in recent memory. We can all take great pride in knowing that Philadelphia was the central reason for his visit to the United States of America. His visit was a unique gift, but it's not relegated to one moment in time. We all have an obligation to embrace the spirit of the visit in an ongoing fashion by taking Pope Francis' example to heart. May it guide each of us to exhibit charity, kindness, compassion, and humility in our daily lives.

I pray that the book you are enjoying will serve as a reminder of Pope Francis' journey to the United States. May it inspire all of us to work toward the transformation of ourselves and our society in deeply positive ways through God's spirit of fellowship and joy.

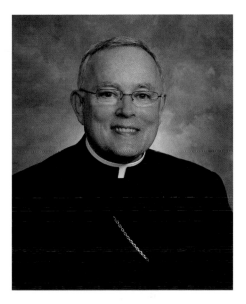

Sincerely,

Most Reverend Charles J. Chaput, O.F.M. Cap.
Archbishop of Philadelphia

Clem Murray / Staff Photographer

# PRELUDE: POPE FRANCIS IN PHILADELPHIA

Projected images light up the dome of the Cathedral Basilica of SS. Peter and Paul to honor the Virgin Mary as the "Undoer of Knots," one of Pope Francis' favorite devotions.

*Tom Gralish /Staff Photographer*

Pilgrims jam the Benjamin Franklin Parkway, waiting for Pope Francis to celebrate the closing Mass of the World Meeting of Families. *Michael Bryant / Staff Photographer*

The Begonia family takes a selfie at Love Park while they wait to see Pope Francis at the Festival of Families. *Joseph Kaczmarek / For The Inquirer*

Michael Woody and Hanley Rice (center) watch the Pope's address at the Festival of Families on a Jumbotron on Broad Street. *Aaron Windhorst / Staff Photographer*

The pontiff kisses a baby at Independence Mall. *David Maialetti / Staff Photographer*

Carefree and car-free, John Smith and son Maxwell enjoy the traffic restrictions imposed on parts of Philadelphia for the pope's visit. *Matthew Hall / For The Inquirer*

Thousands wait to see the pope's motorcade before the Mass on the Parkway. *Bradley C. Bower / For The Inquirer*

The Vance family of Galena, Ohio, 19 strong, kneel to pray and watch on a Jumbotron as Pope Francis celebrates Mass many blocks away. Left to right are Jeremiah Noblet, Lorraine Vance, Gabriel Vance, Rachael Vance and Frank Vance. *Charles Fox / Staff Photographer*

Pope Francis and Archbishop Charles J. Chaput, of Philadelphia, share the sign of peace during Mass on the Parkway. *Clem Murray / Staff Photographer*

Spectators cheer Pope Francis during the Festival of Families on Sept. 26. *Joseph Kaczmarek / For The Inquirer*

Pope Francis arrives at the Festival. *Yong Kim / Staff Photographer*

Here he comes! Pilgrims on the Benjamin Franklin Parkway strain forward as the pope approaches. *Clem Murray / Staff Photographer*

Surrounded by security, Pope Francis waves to the crowd on his way to celebrate Mass. *Clem Murray / Staff Photographer*

Jacen Roberson, 12, holds up a sign he hopes will catch the attention of Pope Francis as the pontiff makes his way down the Ben Franklin Parkway for the Festival of Families.

*Emily Cohen / For The Inquirer*

Good night, all! The pope waves as he leaves the Festival of Families. *Clem Murray / Staff Photographer*

Pope Francis speaks about religious freedom and immigration in an address at Independence Hall. *Elizabeth Robertson / Staff Photographer*

Rosary in hand, Elizabeth Slagley found a treetop vantage point to watch Pope Francis. *Matthew Hall / For The Inquirer*

Students of St. Charles Borromeo Seminary greet Pope Francis as he walks the hallway leading to the seminary chapel, where he would speak to a gathering of bishops. *Tom Gralish / Staff Photographer*

Sister Angeles, of the Eucharistic Guadalupanas of the Heavenly Father wears a traditional habit but her backpack bears a modern message. *Michael Bryant / Staff Photographer*

Pilgrims on North Broad Street wait to enter the secured area during the first day of the pope's visit. *Tom Gralish / Staff Photographer*

Adam Arget Singer and Liza Graziano park their tandem bike for a kiss break on the car-free Benjamin Franklin Bridge on Sept. 26. The span was closed to traffic for security reasons.

*Tom Gralish / Staff Photographer*

Sister Maria Pia (left) and Sister Angeles (right), of the Eucharistic Guadalupanas of the Heavenly Father, hold up a tapestry of Our Lady of Guadalupe outside the World Meeting of Families. The sisters were selling rosary beads to raise money for their work in Colombia. *Michael Bryant / Staff Photographer*

The Black Catholic Community Choir performs at the papal Mass on the Parkway. *Jessica Griffin / Staff Photographer*

Pope Francis preaches during Mass at the Cathedral Basilica of SS. Peter and Paul.

*Clem Murray / Staff Photographer*

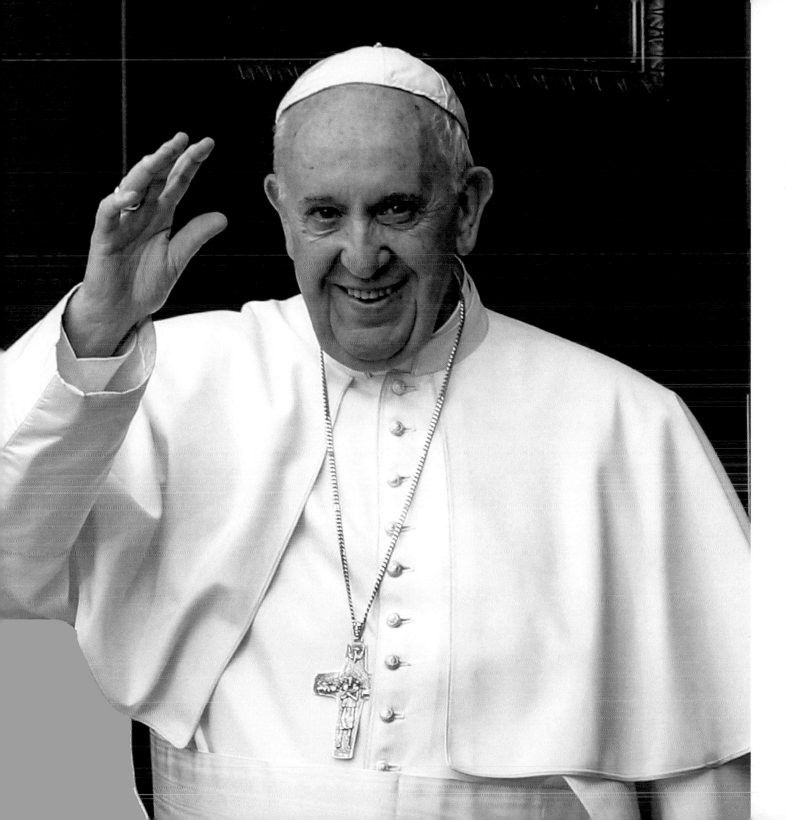

Pope Francis arrives at the Cathedral Basilica for Mass.

*Steven M. Falk / Staff Photographer*

# CHAPTER ONE

# POPE FRANCIS: PROFILE IN COMPASSION

By Austen Ivereigh

Like Americans who explain their origins by starting with their grandparents crossing the Atlantic, Francis — the first pope from the New World — likes to tell how his Piedmontese forebears landed in Argentina in 1929.

Giovanni and Rosa Bergoglio sailed from Genova to Buenos Aires on the *Giulio Cesare* to join his elder brothers, who had done well with their paving firm in the city of Paraná. The couple took with them their only son, Mario, a 20-year-old bank clerk, who would have been astonished to think of himself as the father of a future pope.

---

**OPPOSITE:** Pope Francis speaks to migrants, some wearing white caps, during his visit to the island of Lampedusa on July 8, 2013. The pope traveled to the tiny island south of Sicily to pray for migrants lost at sea. He threw a wreath of flowers into the sea and celebrated Mass as yet another boatload of Eritrean migrants came ashore.

*AP Photo/Alessandra Tarantino, pool*

The figure who always looms largest in Francis' telling is Mario's mother, the Pope's grandmother, Rosa Margarita Vassallo. She was a humble-born, well-read, devout and compassionate woman with finely honed political instincts. List those qualities, and you realize how much of Rosa her grandson has inherited.

She was of peasant stock, and smart as a whip. Sent to Turin at an early age to get a good education, she spoke French and was well-read. Mario — she had five more children, but they were stillborn — took after his mother: He, too, worked hard and did well at school.

Rosa, then in her forties, was a speaker and organizer of events to promote the social teaching of the popes. She more than once clashed with Fascists who saw Catholic Action — a huge network of active lay people across Italy — as a rival to their cadres. One time, when they wouldn't let her speak in a church, she gave the speech in the street on a soapbox. As cardinal, her grandson would do the same many years later in Buenos Aires, speaking through a megaphone in Constitución square.

After marrying in Turin, the Bergoglios moved to the town of Asti when Giovanni came back from the war in 1918. They were due to set sail in October 1927 on the *Principessa Mafalda*, but were forced at the last minute to change their tickets and didn't leave until a year later. It was a lucky escape: the *Mafalda* went down off Brazil, taking more than 300 passengers to their deaths.

The future pope's parents finally made it in February 1929, spending two years in Paraná, a provincial capital northwest of Buenos Aires, before the world recession caused the paving business to founder — and the brothers to separate. Giovanni, Rosa and Mario made their way to Buenos Aires.

"They were out on the street, with nothing," the Pope later recalled. "My grandfather bought a warehouse with 2000 pesos which he borrowed, and my father, who was an accountant, sold goods out of a basket."

Mario met Regina Sívori — the daughter of Genovese immigrants — through their parish, and they married in 1935. A year later, their eldest son Jorge Mario was born, on Dec. 17, 1936, and was baptized a week later, on Christmas Day.

Growing up with the stories of his family's trials and fresh starts, Jorge would always have a special concern for vulnerable migrants. As cardinal, he had a close bond with Paraguayans and Bolivians in the slums of Buenos Aires, and he has made making room for the stranger a cornerstone of his teaching as pope, insisting that anti-immigrant countries that tighten or close borders simply turn nearby oceans and deserts into cemeteries for those who die trying to get there.

To emphasize his deep concern for the plight of desperate migrants, Francis made his first official papal trip outside Rome to the Italian island of Lampedusa, where thousands die trying to cross the Mediterranean from North Africa — "in boats which were vehicles of hope and became vehicles of death."

---

## Profit from the lives, the stories and the wisdom of your elders, of your grandparents.

POPE FRANCIS

The tragedy, he said, "has constantly come back to me like a painful thorn in my heart."

On the eve of his visit to the United States, faced with the continuing tide of refugees fleeing the war in Syria, he asked every church community in Europe to take in refugees — and cleared space in the Vatican to receive two such families.

\*\*\*\*

Jorge, the eldest of five, spent a happy childhood in the barrio of Flores, then on the outskirts of Buenos Aires (today pretty much in the center of the city), where houses were cheap and the streets unpaved. Flores was his home for his first 20

years, in the 1940s and the 1950s; it was where he lived, attended primary school, and worshipped.

By the time Jorge was born, his father was getting bookkeeping work, and could buy a house. Round the corner were Giovanni and Rosa, who looked after him during the day. "My strongest childhood memory is that life shared between my parents' house and my grandparents' house," Francis later recalled.

Rosa would read Piedmontese poetry to him (which he can recite to this day) and introduced him to the classics of Italian literature; she talked of Catholic Action, and the struggle for just wages in Turin. Her piety deeply marked him.

Rosa remained the love of the future Pope's life. Many years later, long after the deaths of his grandfather and father, Francis would visit her in the Buenos Aires nursing home where she was cared for by Italian nuns. "He adored her, she was his weakness," the nuns remembered. They recall the night she died, when Francis, then a Jesuit priest, held her

body until her final breath.

Francis is emphatic about the importance of grandparents. "Profit from the lives, the stories and the wisdom of your elders, of your grandparents," he told young people in Paraguay in July. "'Waste' lots of time listening to all the good things they have to teach you. They are the guardians of that spiritual legacy of faith and values that define a people and light its path."

The Bergoglios were not well-off: they had no car and took no vacations — to this day, the Pope never goes away in the summer — and clothes were recycled. But there was food, education, and strong Italian family solidarity. Jorge was close to his brothers Oscar and Alberto and sisters Marta and María Elena (the only one still alive) and would be a devoted uncle to their children.

Life revolved around the parish, the Basilica of St. Joseph, and the family priest, Salesian Father Enrico Pozzoli, was a regular at table. Another fixed point was San Lorenzo football club stadium, where Mario took his two sons, Jorge and Alberto. For a time, while their mother Regina was ill, the boys were sent to a boarding school, which Jorge loved.

Jorge was a conventional child — tall, lanky, bookish, gentle — who liked to kick a ball and hang out with friends and to dance *milongas*, fast-paced tangos. In high school he

**ABOVE:** Jorge Bergoglio, (left) now Pope Francis, and his brother Oscar.
*File Photos AP/Bergoglio Family Photo*

**OPPOSITE:** An 11-year-old Jorge Bergoglio, now Pope Francis, in his youth in Buenos Aires.
*File Photos AP/Bergoglio Family Photo*

qualified to be a food chemist and also worked in a laboratory, but his best subjects were the humanities.

As an adolescent, three things marked him: his fierce intelligence, his strong religious faith, and his concern for others. But he didn't feel the tug of a vocation until he was almost 17. It came in the confessional, one spring day in 1953, and left him convinced he would eventually be a priest. "It was like being thrown from a horse," he later wrote.

He kept the experience to himself and for the next three years struggled with another calling — to politics.

---

# I didn't lie to you, Mom, I'm going to be a doctor of the soul.

YOUNG JORGE BERGOGLIO

He loved to frequent political clubs and devoured the books lent him by his left-wing Paraguayan boss at the laboratory, the other great female influence on his childhood. Marxism never convinced him, but he would always sympathize with the struggle of political movements for greater social justice.

The vocation to the priesthood eventually won out. His mother Regina, whom he had told he was studying to be a doctor, was shocked to discover theology books in his room. "I didn't lie to you, Mom," he told her. "I'm going to be a doctor of the soul." Regina was appalled, and refused to support his decision for many years. But his father and grandparents backed him.

At 20, a year after entering the seminary in Buenos Aires in March 1956, he nearly died from a devastating pleurisy, painful inflamed lung membranes, that led to the surgical removal of three pulmonary cysts and part of his right lung. To this day, Pope Francis speaks softly, gets breathless and suffers often from chest conditions.

After recovering he joined the Jesuits, a missionary religious order renowned for its intellectual rigor and long formation — the detailed process of becoming a Jesuit priest. In March 1958, Jorge began his 14 years of training, initially in Córdoba and Santiago, in neighboring Chile, but mostly in the place that was to be his home for most of his life until the mid-1980s: the huge Jesuit formation house, or college, an hour outside Buenos Aires, known as the Colegio Máximo.

****

Jorge Bergoglio's long period of study and formation as a Jesuit coincided with great turbulence in both the church and in politics, shaped above all by the Second Vatican Council and the Cuban Revolution. He identified with a group of theologians and thinkers who stood outside the sharp divisions of the era between left and right, conservative and progressive.

Those in the "La Plata school," as it is sometimes called, were nationalists who looked to the tradition of Peronism, a uniquely Argentine blend of Catholic social teaching and pro-worker, populist ideas that rejected both liberalism and communism as alien. To this day, Pope Francis has a fierce sense of the importance of the values of the *patria*, or homeland. When Argentina celebrated the bicentenary of its independence in 2010, then-Cardinal Bergoglio wrote that while a country's borders and much else can change, "the *patria* either preserves its foundational being or it dies."

With this nationalism went a strong notion that Jesus Christ evangelizes in and through the culture of a people — and that people become free when they are able to resist what is imposed on that culture from the outside. In

Manila in January 2015, for example, Francis spoke powerfully of the need for the developing world to resist the "ideological colonization" of gay marriage and abortion.

In the 1970s he was critical of Latin American theologians who looked to (foreign, Marxist-influenced) social sciences as a means of "liberating" the poor. Although initially supportive of the national and popular Cuban revolution in 1959, Bergoglio's group was horrified when Fidel Castro declared the Revolution to be Marxist, and fell into the Soviet orbit.

For Bergoglio and the La Plata school, the task of the church was to build up the culture of the people, so that they could become protagonists in their own liberation. This meant looking to the cultural traditions of ordinary people, valuing, for example, popular forms of devotion that the more intellectual Jesuits looked down on as superstitious. It was in some ways a conservative outlook, yet in other ways radical, because it was rooted in ordinary people and was suspicious of elites of both right and left who tried to speak in the people's name.

In all the turbulence, the Jesuits were hit hard by a sudden drop in vocations and an exodus of many priests. In the midst of deep divisions over the direction of the Jesuits in Argentina, Bergoglio in 1973 was chosen to lead its 450 men at the age of just 36. His deep spirituality and leadership skills had made a deep impression. He was considered the right man for the delicate task of uniting the Jesuits and carrying through reforms that would hold to what was essential while making necessary changes. That would be his mandate, too, as Pope, decades later.

He was too young for the responsibility, as he would later admit, and made many mistakes. He was too authoritarian in his leadership, and suffered from a weakness typical of charismatic leaders — of creating a cult of personality. He was the most brilliant and successful leader the Argentine Jesuits had ever had. By the end of his six-year term (1973-79), the Colegio Máximo had filled up with dozens of new vocations attracted by his compelling vision of radical service and deep spirituality, one that stayed clear of ideology while focusing the Jesuit men on the concrete needs and values of the people they were serving. He did all this during a period of horrific guerrilla violence followed by a brutal military dictatorship.

Sympathizing with neither the leftists nor the army, Bergoglio managed to steer the Jesuits through the turbulent 1970s without losing any of his men. One Jesuit said later: "He was our storm pilot." Famous for being inscrutable — his Jesuit nickname was *La Giaconda*, the Italian name for the Mona Lisa — Bergoglio always played his cards close to his chest. (It is a characteristic of his leadership as pope: few in Rome know what Francis is thinking, or what he will do next.) He managed to help dozens of people fleeing military repression, hiding them in the Colegio and helping them escape the country — all under the noses of the army and the Jesuit military chaplains. These stories would only come out later, after he was made pope, dispelling the myth that grew up around him in the 1980s — and repeated later by his enemies—that he had "collaborated" with the military regime.

In 1980 he was appointed to a six-year term as rector, or head, of the Colegio Máximo. There he created an extraordinary regime: austere, disciplined, but highly motivated, with dedicated young Jesuits whose energetic pastoral work with the poor transformed the town of San Miguel, where the Colegio is located. In practice, he remained the leader of the Jesuits, adored by a whole new generation who looked to him. No one disputes his brilliance as a leader — "a mixture of Machiavelli and a desert saint", as one Jesuit once said. But his overwhelming influence divided opinion among the older Jesuits, who were concerned at his hold over the young.

They successfully lobbied the new Jesuit general in Rome to have him and his followers removed from positions of influence. After the end of his term as rector, in 1986, Bergoglio and those closest to him were sent abroad, but he came back after six months in Germany for reasons that have never really been clarified.

After years of turbulence, Bergoglio was sent into a kind of internal exile, in the mountain city of Córdoba, where he spent the years 1990-91 hearing confessions and ministering to elderly, sick Jesuits. Deprived suddenly of authority, and watching the province he loved split into factions, he suffered intensely. He was often sick and depressed, but mostly it was a time of deep prayer and contemplation that bore fruit in some of his most powerful writings. The Córdoba exile was a radical purgation that left Bergoglio humbler, gentler, and more compassionate.

It also brought to an end his time with the Jesuits, although he technically remained a member of the order.

***

In 1992, for the second but not the last time, Bergoglio appeared out of nowhere to take up a position of major responsibility. Very few in the archdiocese of Buenos Aires had even heard of him when he was made an auxiliary bishop, serving under the city's new cardinal, Antonio Quarracino. He was back in the area of the city he had grown up in, one that included many of the city's shantytowns and sanctuaries.

Bishop Bergoglio deeply impressed his clergy by his directness, humility and compassion. He established habits, many carried over from his days as a Jesuit, that he keeps up to this day: rising at 4.30 a.m. to spend two hours in prayer, maintaining his own diary and making his own calls, taking a 40-minute siesta in the afternoon, and retiring early at night, at about 10 p.m. Between those hours, he has always worked intensely, never taking time off or even vacations. (As pope, he has refused the summer break at the papal summer palace of Castelgandolfo, instead opening it to the public.)

Just as he does now as pope, as bishop he kept his own diary and made his own calls, traveling on foot or on public transport, always there for his priests. Refusing all requests for interviews, he was barely visible on the public stage, even after Cardinal Quarracino made him vicar-general, one of the most senior positions in the archdiocese.

In June 1997 he was made "coadjutor archbishop", meaning that he would automatically become

**ABOVE:** Pope Benedict XVI, right, embraces Cardinal Jorge Bergoglio at a meeting of Latin American bishops in Brazil in 2007.

*AP Photo/Ricardo Mazalan*

**ABOVE:** Austen Ivereigh (and wife Linda) presenting his book to Pope Francis. *Osservatore Romano*

**OPPOSITE:** Pope Francis joins surprised Vatican workers at lunch in their cafeteria in July 2014. The pope waited in line for his lunch of pasta, cod and grilled tomatoes, but the cashier didn't have the courage to charge him when he got to the register. *Osservatore Romano*

emerged as a national figure above all during the economic and political collapse of 2002, when Argentina defaulted on its debt, the government fell, and overnight half of the country was made unemployed.

Cardinal Bergoglio mobilized the city to help the jobless, homeless and destitute, turning the church's parishes and projects into shelters and feeding stations. It was here that he was able to implement his vision of a "Samaritan Church" that later as pope he described as a "battlefield hospital", one focused on the needs and suffering of people. Drawing on decades of prayer and spiritual guidance, Cardinal Bergoglio was convinced that when people experience the mercy of God — in the form of unconditional forgiveness, total acceptance, or acts of compassion — they encounter the true face of God, and have their hearts and minds opened. For Cardinal Bergoglio, as for Pope Francis now, exercising mercy and charity is the same as evangelization.

Bergoglio emerged in those years as the champion of ordinary Argentines, holding to account Argentina's politicians on their behalf. Journalists eagerly looked forward to the annual patriotic service of blessing of the nation and its leaders to hear the cardinal excoriate the political class for its detachment and its lack of attention to ordinary people — just as he would later do as pope when addressing the

the European Parliament or the U.S. Congress. Eventually, a new government led by the insecure and anticlerical President Néstor Kirchner would veto those cathedral celebrations, which only made Bergoglio look even stronger.

This was Bergoglio exercising religious freedom, a liberty he regards as key to the flourishing of all societies: for the church to critique and hold to account the state and economic leaders on behalf of the voiceless, according to the values and standards of the culture. He did not see it as the task of bishops to bring down governments, but to connect them with the concerns and values of the people. Build politics, he told Bolivian leaders in July 2015, "on the real needs and on the lived experience of your brothers and sisters."

At the 2005 conclave to elect the successor to Pope John Paul II, Cardinal Bergoglio found himself in the Sistine Chapel for the first time in his life. He was in for another surprise, attracting votes as the alternative to Cardinal Joseph Ratzinger, who would become Pope Benedict XVI. He was shocked at the prospect, for which he felt spiritually unprepared, and begged the other cardinals to desist. But the fact that something like a fifth of them had voted for him was a sign that his reputation, despite his best efforts at avoiding attention, had been quietly spreading.

Archbishop of Buenos Aires upon Quarracino's death. Quarracino died in March the following year.

Yet again, nobody quite knew who this Bergoglio was; journalists described him as austere and well-liked, but allergic to interviews. Even in 2001, when he was made a cardinal by Pope John Paul II, he stayed mostly in the shadows, giving only brief answers in his first interview.

But over the next two years Buenos Aires grew to love its cardinal, who

OPPOSITE: Pope Francis arrives
in St Peter's Square at the Vatican
for the weekly papal audience.

*David Maialetti / Staff Photographer*

***

The other key moment in his journey to the papacy came two years later, when the bishops from Latin America came together for a historic assembly, the first of its kind in 15 years. The 2007 meeting in Aparecida, Brazil, marked the coming of age of the Latin American Church, and above all of the La Plata school, whose ideas underpin the document that emerged from it.

Cardinal Bergoglio was the driving force of Aparecida, elected unanimously to take charge of the process that led to the document. His performance and homilies led many Latin American cardinals to regard him from that time as a future pope.

Yet for the next five years, Cardinal Bergoglio remained focused on his diocese, trying to leave it as little as possible. ("I don't like to leave my spouse for too long", he would say) and going to Rome only when he had to. These were years in which he began to display extraordinary courage: organizing destitute workers, challenging corrupt police chiefs and politicians, confronting drug merchants and freeing trafficked migrants. He refused all invitations to dinner parties and functions in the wealthy part of Buenos Aires, preferring to spend his weekends in the shantytowns. He became deeply concerned by the destruction left by unrestrained market capitalism, and the power of global corporations: fracking for natural gas in Patagonia and paper-making at a mill in Uruguay that contaminated the town of Gualeguaychú also became concerns at this time.

They were also years in which he developed deep friendships with leaders of other faiths and denominations and experienced something of a conversion to charismatic forms of prayer, gathering to meet each month with five evangelical pastors. Yet most to take part in the conclave. Little known in the European media, and assumed to be too old, he was barely considered a candidate in the weeks before the election. But the cardinals who knew him well believed he was the man of the hour, and pointed to him as an austere reformer with the political savvy to reform the dysfunctions of the Vatican and energize the world's Church.

On the eve of the conclave, the Argentine Jesuit stood to address his

---

## I don't like to leave my spouse for too long.

CARDINAL BERGOGLIO

---

of this activity was not widely known. Although he allowed himself to be interviewed for a 2010 book-length profile of him, *El Jesuita*, Bergoglio hardly ever spoke to the press. When he was elected pope in 2013, there was very little for the world's media to work off.

In 2011, he made preparations for his retirement — he would turn 75 the following year — on the assumption he would be replaced as archbishop in 2012. But there were other plans.

In February 2013, after Pope Benedict's epoch-making announcement that he would retire, Cardinal Bergoglio made his way to Rome fellow cardinals in a brief but powerful speech that convinced many of them that God had already chosen the next pope. It contained his key ideas: the importance of the Church focusing on the "peripheries" — the places of exclusion and suffering — as well as its duty to evangelize.

As happened so often before, when he emerged on the balcony of St Peter's on the night of March 13, 2013, joking that that his brother cardinals had had to go to the ends of the earth to find a new pope, few in the media or the crowds below knew who he was.

They would soon find out.

♦

# CHAPTER TWO

# CUBA

A cannon salute, a marching band, and bolts of lightning welcomed Pope Francis to Cuba as he arrived on Sept. 19 for the first leg of a remarkably ambitious pair of pastoral visits to Cuba and the United States. Waiting for him on the tarmac of José Martí Airport was President Raul Castro.

"I love the Cuban people," the Argentine-born pope told journalists on the 12-hour flight from Rome to Havana.

Early in the visit, Francis paid a private visit to Castro's older brother Fidel, 89, the aging, ailing lion of the Cuban Revolution. Along with books by two Cuban Catholic thinkers — one of them an instructor of Castro's — the pontiff gave Castro a copy of *Laudato Si'*, his recent encyclical admonishing the world's wealthy that environmental depredation is a moral wrong that gravely oppresses the poor.

Since Francis' election in March 2013, his concern for the poor and marginalized has evidently resounded with Raul Castro, so much that the long-marginalized Catholic Church appears to be enjoying new esteem. The pope is credited with initiating the private talks that led to recently restored diplomatic relations between the United States and Cuba.

Dressed in a suit and tie, Raul Castro attended the Mass that Francis celebrated Sunday in Plaza de la Revolución. And when he and Francis exited Plaza de la Revolución after a private talk, Castro clutched the pope's hand at length and repeatedly patted his arm.

---

**OPPOSITE:** Pope Francis and Fidel Castro meet at Castro's residence on Sept. 20. The 40-minute meeting, described by the Vatican as informal and familial, included an exchange of books. *Alex Castro / Associated Press*

**ABOVE:** A crowd watches the pope approach on his way to San Cristobal Cathedral in Havana on Sept. 20. The pontiff finished his day with a Vespers service at the cathedral and a meeting with Cuban youth. *Desmond Boylan / Associated Press*

**RIGHT:** Under the gaze of Cuban revolutionary icon Che Guevara, Pope Francis approaches the altar to celebrate Mass in Havana's Revolution Square on Sept. 20. *Tony Gentile / Reuters / Pool*

**OPPOSITE:** Pope Francis makes his way to the Metropolitan Cathedral in Santiago de Cuba on Sept. 22. The pope called on Cubans to rediscover their Catholic heritage and live a "revolution of tenderness." *Ramon Espinosa / Associated Press*

# CHAPTER THREE

# WASHINGTON, D.C.

The event was unprecedented, the message groundbreaking, and the audience rapt. Never before had a pope ventured to Capitol Hill, standing in the well of American political power, acknowledging the nation's achievements while challenging its leaders to do more — and do better.

In a sweeping call to "the common good and cooperation," Pope Francis used his historic Sept. 24 address to strike themes of compassion and peace, applying age-old religious teachings to some of the most charged policy debates of the era.

Reinforcing his reputation as a caretaker for the poor, the pontiff abstained from the typical power lunch after his address, and instead visited the homeless and needy at an event and lunch with Catholic Charities workers outside a Washington church.

The Pope stepped into some of America's most contested debates the day before as President Obama welcomed him to the White House. In his remarks to the President, Pope Francis called for action on climate change and sympathy for immigrants. Later that that day, the Pope met with U.S. bishops and urged them to avoid "harsh and divisive" language. And in a ceremony before thousands at the Basilica of the National Shrine of the Immaculate Conception, he presided over the first-ever canonization ceremony in the United States, elevating to sainthood Junipero Serra, a Franciscan missionary who helped spread the faith to California in the 1700s.

---

**OPPOSITE:** Pope Francis addresses a joint session of Congress on Sept. 24, the first pope ever to do so. *Evan Vucci / Associated Press*

**ABOVE RIGHT:** President Barack Obama and First Lady Michelle Obama introduce Pope Francis to their dogs, Sunny and Bo, at the White House.

*Pete Souza / White House Photographer*

**BELOW RIGHT:** Pope Francis arrives after his address to Congress at a lunch for homeless people who are regularly fed at St. Patrick's Church in Washington, D.C.

*L'Osservatore Romano / Pool photo via AP*

**OPPOSITE:** The pope, accompanied by Vice President Biden and members of Congress, greets a crowd gathered outside the Capitol.

*Doug Mills / The New York Times via AP, pool*

# CHAPTER FOUR

# NEW YORK

H e followed a path taken by his predecessors, but the message was all his own.

As Pope Francis appeared before the United Nations General Assembly on Sept. 25, he hailed the U.N.'s role in promoting human rights, peacekeeping, and advancing the rule of law, and he urged its member nations to do more to protect the environment and the world's neediest.

Before an audience of world leaders, the pontiff amplified the themes he struck during his nine-day North American pastoral journey. Speaking in his native Spanish, his message was more fluid — and at times more pointed — than the historic address he gave to Congress a day earlier.

Despite its good work and worthy goals, Francis reminded the General Assembly, there are "many victims of badly exercised power." He cited two: the environment and the very poor.

"These sectors are closely interconnected, and made increasingly fragile by dominant political and economic relationships," he said. "Their rights must be forcefully affirmed, by working to protect the environment and by putting an end to exclusion."

The U.N. visit marked the first stop on an itinerary that carried the pope to disparate but significant destinations across the nation's largest city. He led an interfaith service at the 9/11 memorial and met with relatives of the Sept. 11 attack's victims, visited a school in East Harlem, paraded by motorcade through Central Park, and ended the day with a Mass at Madison Square Garden.

**OPPOSITE:** Pope Francis lays a white rose at the South Pool of the 9/11 Memorial at Ground Zero in New York before an interfaith prayer service on Sept. 25. *John Minchillo / Associated Press*

**ABOVE:** The pope passes among members of the Young People's Chorus of New York City after the prayer service at the 9/11 Memorial and Museum.

*Ray Stubblebine / Pool / Getty Images*

**OPPOSITE:** Pope Francis celebrates Mass at Madison Square Garden on Sept. 25. *Michael Appleton / Pool / Getty Images*

# CHAPTER FIVE

# PHILADELPHIA

Hundreds of thousands of people packed Philadelphia's Benjamin Franklin Parkway to see and hear Pope Francis celebrate Mass in the glorious finale to a historic two-day visit by a pontiff who spoke loudly for tolerance, brotherhood, and peace.

The huge ceremony at the foot of the Philadelphia Museum of Art steps was a moving, religious tribute from a pope who, while here, directly addressed the sick, desperate, and needy.

"Faith grows when it is lived and shaped by love," a visibly weary Francis said in his homily. The pope, 78, had been in almost constant, morning-to-night movement since his arrival.

A hush followed the pope's words, as if all of Philadelphia had paused. The quiet was broken only by the cries of children made cranky by crowds and long lines.

Scores of nuns and priests looked on. Children perched on their fathers' shoulders. People of different ethnicities and cultures stood side by side: suburbanites who had battled their way into the city; missionary-driven faithful who had traveled from distant nations to see a beloved pope.

As the crowd strained forward to see the pope, Lina Naula handed her month-old son Matthew to Kristin Heinly, a stranger standing in front of her, in the hope that Pope Francis would notice the child. He did. A security agent carried the baby to the pontiff, who bent to Matthew, kissed him and blessed him.

---

**OPPOSITE:** Pope Francis celebrates the closing Mass of the World Meeting of Families on the Benjamin Franklin Parkway. *Yong Kim / Staff Photographer*

**RIGHT:** Pilgrims from southern Alabama trundle their luggage into the Aquinas Center in South Philadelphia, where they will be staying during the pope's visit. *Clem Murray / Staff Photographer*

**OPPOSITE LEFT:** Participants in the World Meeting of Families crowd an escalator at the Pennsylvania Convention Center on their way to an afternoon session on Sept. 24. *Ed Hille / Staff Photographer*

**OPPOSITE TOP RIGHT:** It's football and conversation on the Parkway the day before the pope's arrival. *David Swanson / Staff Photographer*

**OPPOSITE BOTTOM RIGHT:** Before the opening ceremony of the World Meeting of Families on Sept. 22, Archbishop Vincenzo Paglia, president of the Pontifical Council for the Family (second from right), keeps the moment light with Donna Crilley Farrell, WMOF executive director (left); Robert J. Ciaruffoli, WMOF president (second from left); Archbishop Charles J. Chaput (center) and Mayor Michael A. Nutter (right). *David Maialetti / Staff Photographer*

**BELOW:** Ernesto Zamora and other members of the Mariachi Lupita from St. Mary's Parish in East Chicago, Ind., practice for a performance they plan to give on the Parkway while waiting for Pope Francis. Their parish is largely Mexican, many of them undocumented, and families often face harassment over immigration issues. *Matthew Hall / For The Inquirer*

**ABOVE:** A platoon of pope bobbleheads raise their hands in blessing. *Stephanie Aaronson / Staff Photographer*

**RIGHT:** The colors of the American flag provide the backdrop for a pope T-shirt. *Matthew Hall / For The Inquirer*

**BELOW:** New Philly guy Pope Francis joins longtime local favorites Ben Franklin and Rocky Balboa on the shelf at a souvenir shop. *Tom Gralish / Staff Photographer*

**LEFT:** The entrepreneurial spirit was strong as souvenir shops in Philadelphia stocked up on pope mementoes in advance of the papal visit. *Tom Gralish / Staff Photographer*

**BELOW:** Getting into the spirit of the papal visit, Andre Davis stands outside the Varga Bar at 10th and Spruce Streets. *Wanda Thomas / Staff Photographer*

**ABOVE:** Thomas Conroy attaches a ribbon to a line at the Knots Grotto.
*David Swanson / Staff Photographer*

**RIGHT:** Two participants in the World Meeting of Families write their prayer requests on ribbons to be hung in the pop-up grotto honoring "Mary, Undoer of Knots," outside the Cathedral Basilica of SS. Peter and Paul.
*Tom Gralish / Staff Photographer*

**OPPOSITE TOP:** The Fitzgibbon family from County Kerry, Ireland, stops for a chat with Philadelphia mounted police officer Paul Tinneny and his horse outside the Reading Terminal Market. *Ed Hille / Staff Photographer*

**OPPOSITE BOTTOM LEFT:** A minivan with Arizona tags asks motorists to put their horn where their heart is. *Charles Fox / Staff Photographer*

**OPPOSITE BOTTOM RIGHT:** In the early evening of Sept. 25, with major highways soon to close in anticipation of the pope's arrival, a lone vehicle heads toward the Benjamin Franklin Bridge. *Elizabeth Robertson / Staff Photographer*

**OPPOSITE TOP LEFT:** With the Ben Franklin Bridge closed to traffic, local residents turn the span into what some were calling "one long block party." *Tom Gralish / Staff Photographer*

**OPPOSITE TOP RIGHT:** Pennsylvania State Police march along the Parkway before the papal Mass as Philadelphia police watch. *David Swanson / Staff Photographer*

**OPPOSITE BOTTOM LEFT:** Students from the Canyon Heights Academy in Campbell, Calif., prepare to board a commuter train at the Pennbrook Station in Lansdale Borough on their way to see Pope Francis. *Mark C. Psoras / For The Inquirer*

**OPPOSITE BOTTOM RIGHT:** Members of the Bishop Shanahan High School marching band practice for their performance at the pope's arrival. *Charles Fox / Staff photographer*

**ABOVE LEFT:** Pope Francis, greets Philadelphia Archbishop Charles Chaput and others as he arrives at Atlantic Aviation in Philadelphia on Sept. 26. *Charles Fox / Staff Photographer*

**LEFT:** Joseph Neubauer, former Aramark Corp. CEO, shakes hands with Pope Francis as Independence Blue Cross president and CEO Daniel Hilferty and his wife, Joan, look on. *Joe Gidjunis / World Meeting of Families*

**FAR LEFT:** Pope Francis waves as he gets off the plane. *Charles Fox / Staff Photographer*

**TOP RIGHT:** Kristin Keating breaks into tears as Pope Francis blesses her son Michael, 10, after arriving at Atlantic Aviation. Michael has cerebral palsy. His father, Chuck, the director of the Bishop Shanahan band, is at the left. *Charles Fox / Staff Photographer*

**BELOW RIGHT:** Pope Francis kisses Michael Keating. The pope spotted Michael as he was about to leave Atlantic Aviation and had his driver stop.

*Joseph Gidjunis / World Meeting of Families via AP*

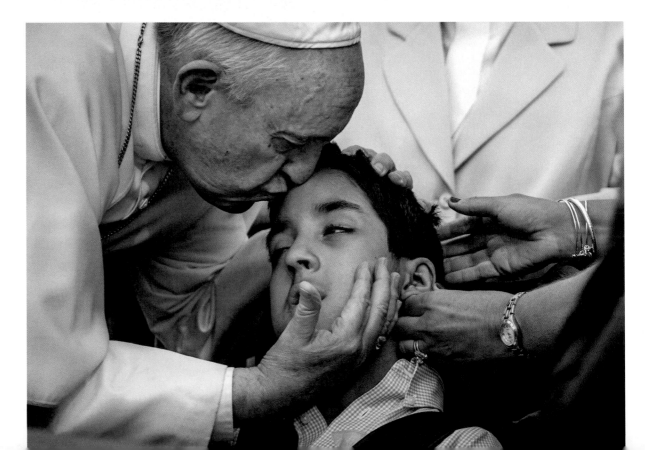

**LEFT:** The pope arrives at the Cathedral Basilica of SS. Peter and Paul on Sept. 26. Former Pennsylvania Gov. Tom Corbett is at the right. *Steven M. Falk / Staff Photographer*

**BELOW:** Sister Eunice Marie, religious education director at SS. Philip and James School in Exton, is elated as Pope Francis celebrates Mass in the Cathedral Basilica on Sept. 26. Sister Eunice is a member of the Sisters, Servants of the Immaculate Heart of Mary, the order that operates Immaculata University. *Bradley C. Bower / Staff Photographer*

**ABOVE:** Pope Francis enters the Cathedral Basilica to celebrate Mass with clergy and religious order members from Pennsylvania. *Jonathan Wilson / For The Inquirer*

**FAR LEFT:** Priests use their cellphones to take pictures as Pope Francis celebrates Mass in the Cathedral Basilica. *Clem Murray / Staff Photographer*

**LEFT:** Occupying the chair normally used by Archbishop Chaput, Pope Francis celebrates Mass. *Clem Murray / Staff Photographer*

**BELOW LEFT:** Archbishop Chaput holds aloft a chalice that Pope Francis gave him during Mass. *Clem Murray / Staff Photographer*

**BELOW:** The pope greets parishioners after Mass. *Bradley C.bower / For The Inquirer*

**ABOVE:** Singers from Dar es Salaam, Tanzania, perform as the crowd assembles for the pope's speech at Independence Hall. *Matthew Hall / For The Inquirer*

**RIGHT:** The pope stops to kiss another baby on his way to Independence Hall. *Ed Hille / Staff Photographer*

**OPPOSITE:** The pope rolls past the site of the President's House on Independence Mall. *Ed Hille / Staff Photographer*

**TOP:** Silvina Rios, of Philadelphia, cries tears of joy as she waits for Pope Francis' arrival at Independence Hall. *David Maialetti / Staff Photographer*

**ABOVE:** Angela Veron smiles as she listens to Pope Francis speak.

*Joseph Kaczmarek / For The Inquirer*

**ABOVE RIGHT:** Natali Quintuna embraces her mother, Miriam Pulla, as they watch the pope on a video monitor. *David Maialetti / Staff Photographer*

**RIGHT:** Darryl Tocco, of Lindenwold, peers through a monocular in an attempt to catch a glimpse of the pope. *Matthew Hall / For The Inquirer*

**OPPOSITE:** Speaking from the lectern Abraham Lincoln used for the Gettysburg Address, Pope Francis delivers a plea for religious freedom.

*Elizabeth Robertson / Staff Photographer*

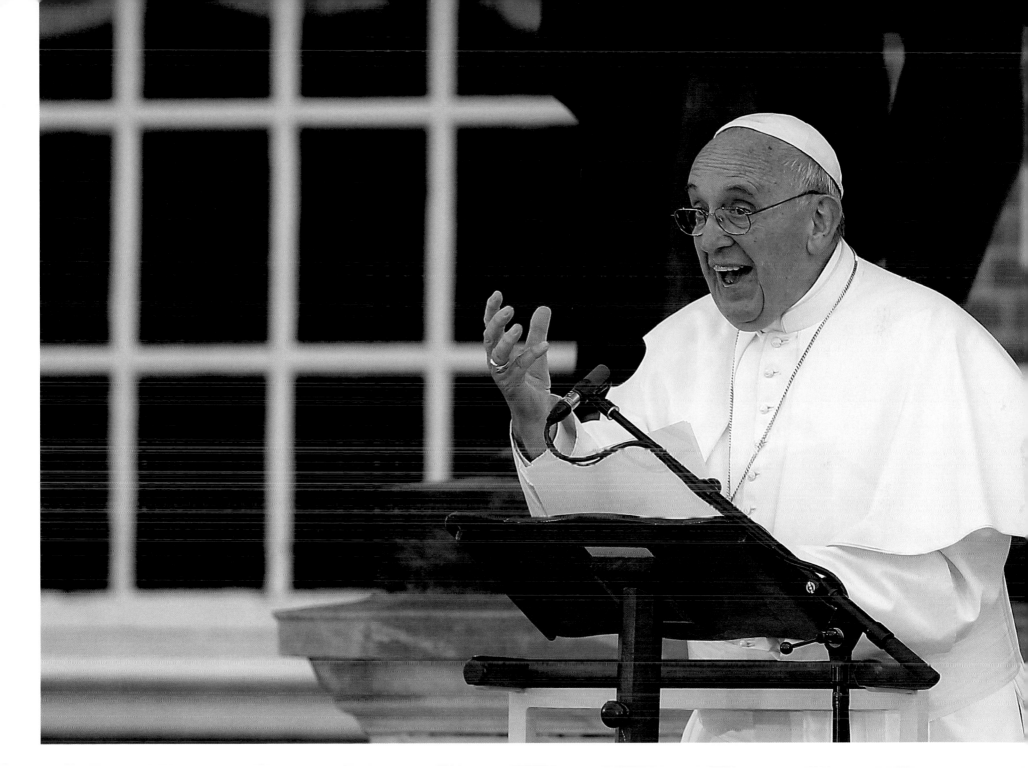

**ABOVE:** The crowd watches on a video monitor as Pope Francis makes his way toward them. *David Maialetti / Staff Photographer*

**LEFT:** Pope Francis and his party are all smiles after the pope stopped to kiss four-month-old Quinn Madden, decked out in a tiny miter.

*Anne Hartman / Archdiocese of Philadelphia*

**OPPOSITE:** Pilgrims hold up religious items as they wait for the pope at Independence Hall. *Davaid Maialetti / Staff Photographer*

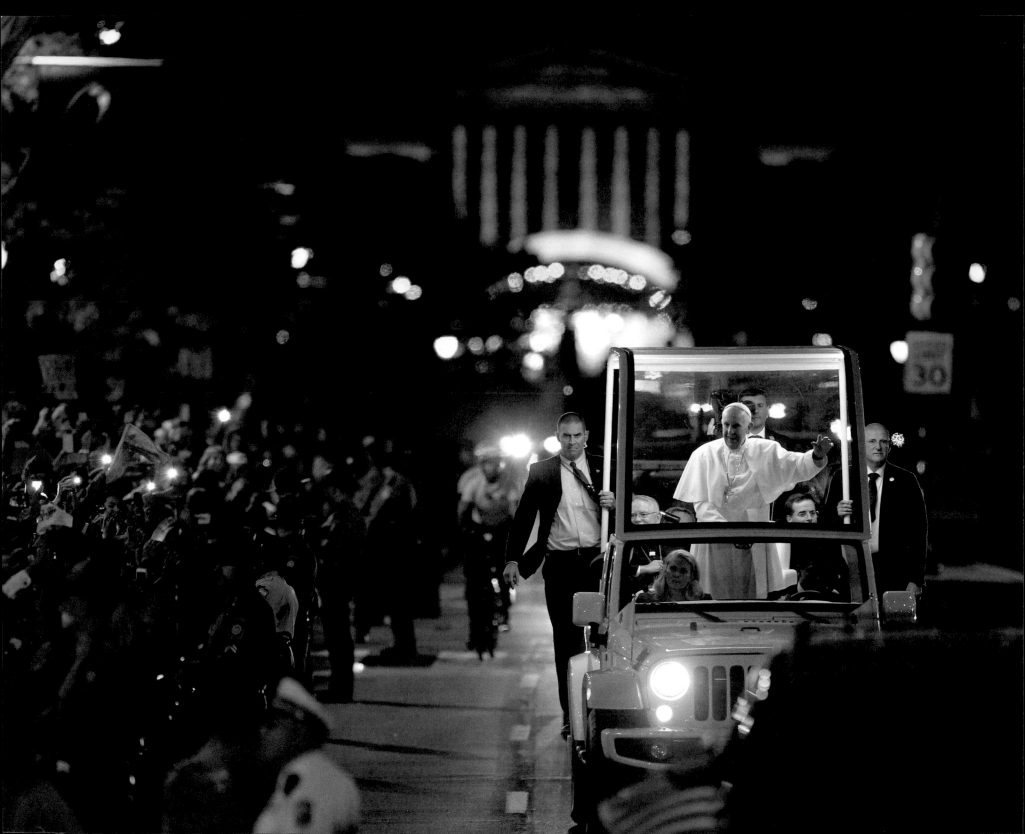

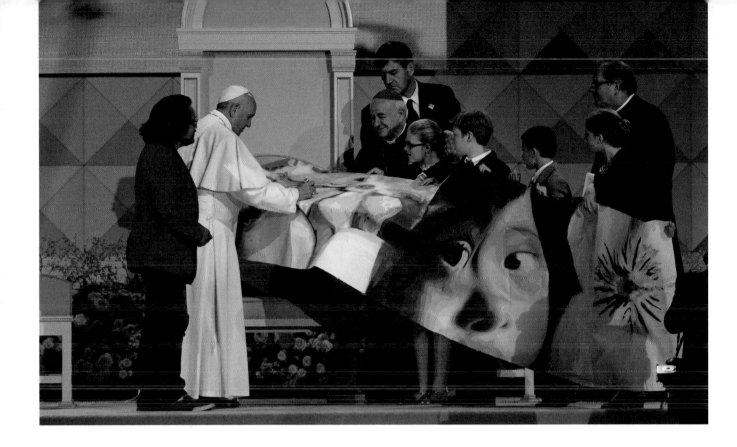

**ABOVE LEFT:** Pope Francis paints the final brush strokes and signs his name to the final panel of a mural painted by more than 2,700 people in honor of the World Meeting of Families 2015 and the pope's visit to Philadelphia. The mural will be installed at Saint Malachy School. *Clem Murray / Staff Photographer*

**BELOW LEFT:** Yannick Nézet-Séguin conducts the Philadelphia Orchestra during the Festival of Families. *Yong Kim / Staff Photographer*

**OPPOSITE:** The flashing lights of security vehicles add dramatic effect to the papal parade at the Festival of Families. *Michael Bryant / Staff Photographer*

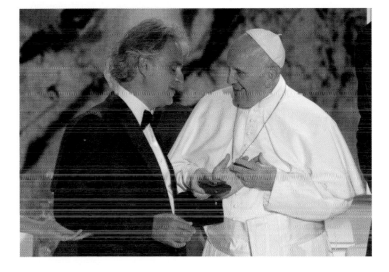

**ABOVE:** Bobby Hill, 14, of Philadelphia, with the Keystone State Boychoir, sang a flawless and spontaneous *a cappella* rendition of Pie Jesu for Pope Francis. *Clem Murray / Staff Photographer*

**ABOVE LEFT:** The Queen of Soul, Aretha Franklin, sings "Amazing Grace." *Yong Kim / Staff Photographer*

**MIDDLE LEFT:** The pope chats with singer Andrea Bocelli, who performed at the Festival.
*Yong Kim / Staff Photographer*

**BELOW LEFT:** Nuns enjoy themselves at the Festival. *Yong Kim / Staff Photographer*

**OPPOSITE:** Pope Francis and Archbishop Chaput applaud dancers from the Pennsylvania Ballet who performed at the Festival. *Clem Murray / Staff Photographer*

**ABOVE RIGHT:** Pope Francis delivers a rousing pep talk on the value of family. *Yong Kim / Staff Photographer*

**BELOW RIGHT:** Colombian rock star Juanes performs during the Festival. *Yong Kim / Staff Photographer*

**OPPOSITE:** Pope Francis greets clergy and seminarians on his arrival at Saint Charles Borromeo Seminary in Wynnewood. *Alejandro A. Alvarez / Staff Photographer*

**ABOVE:** Pope Francis greets seminarians in a hallway of St. Charles Borromeo Seminary. Behind him are Bishop Timothy C. Senior, rector of the seminary (left), and Archbishop Charles J. Chaput (right). *Tom Gralish / Staff Photographer*

**OPPOSITE:** Pope Francis greets the audience assembled to hear his address to a gathering of bishops at the seminary.

*Alejandro A. Alvarez / Staff Photographer*

**RIGHT:** The pope poses with students and faculty of St. Charles Borromeo Seminary outside St. Martin of Tours Chapel. Archbishop Chaput is to the pope's right and Bishop Senior to his left.

*Tom Gralish / Staff Photographer*

**LEFT:** Excitement is the order of the day for the pope's visit to the seminary. *Tom Gralish / Staff Photographer*

**BELOW:** Philadelphia police officers take their own pictures of the pope's group photo with the seminarians.

*Tom Gralish / Staff Photographer*

**TOP LEFT:** Pope Francis greets inmates from across the Philadelphia prison system, selected to meet him at Curran-Fromhold Correctional Facility. *David Maialetti / Staff Photographer*

**BELOW LEFT:** The prisoners listen as the pope speaks. *Charles Fox / Staff Photographer*

**OPPOSITE TOP LEFT:** Inmates Rameen Perrin (left), Evan Davis (center) and Hakiem Burke work on a chair that inmates in the prison system's PhilaCor furniture-making program built for the pope's visit. *Alejandro A. Alvarez / Staff Photographer*

**OPPOSITE BOTTOM LEFT:** The chair-builders show off their work. *Alejandro A. Alvarez / Staff Photographer*

**OPPOSITE RIGHT:** Pope Francis gives a thumbs-up to the prisoners' work. "The chair is beautiful," the pope said. *Charles Fox / Staff Photographer*

**ABOVE:** Pope Francis hugs inmate Luis Zacarias.

*Charles Fox / Staff Photographer*

**OPPOSITE:** The pope greets prisoners during his visit to Curran-Fromhold. *David Maialetti, Staff Photographer*

**TOP RIGHT:** Sister Mary Scullion presents Pope Francis a stole knit with the prayer knots from prisoners, homeless and mentally ill as he visited the Knotted Grotto outside the Cathedral Basilica of SS. Peter and Paul. *Mari A. Schaefer / Staff*

**BELOW RIGHT:** Mayor Nutter runs down the row slappng hands with members of the Philadelphia Boys Choir before the outdoor Papal Mass on the Benjamin Franklin Parkway.

*Clem Murray / Staff Photographer*

**ABOVE:** Wawa convenience store workers struggle to get through the crowd at 17th Street and the Parkway as they carry meals to first responders prior to Mass. *Elizabeth Robertson / Staff Photographer*

**ABOVE:** Pope Francis waves to the pilgrims as the Pope mobile rounds Logan Square on the way to Mass. *Clem Murray / Staff Photographer*

**RIGHT:** Doug and Julie Bauman wear their own version of papal headgear.

*David Swanson / Staff Photographer*

**FAR RIGHT:** Pope Francis leans out of the pope mobile to kiss a crying infant before Mass. *Clem Murray / Staff Photographer*

**RIGHT:** The view of the parkway and Pope Francis' Mass as seen from the Top of the Towers Restaurant at 3 Logan Square.

*Ed Hille / Staff Photographer*

**LEFT:** Sister Mercy Egbeji, of Pittsburgh, waits for Pope Francis to celebrate Mass.
*David Swanson / Staff Photographer*

**FAR LEFT:** A papal smile and a hand raised in blessing, trademarks of a popular pope.
*Clem Murray / Staff Photographer*

**BELOW LEFT:** As awe-struck as if he were right in front of them, Connie Broell (left) and Lindsey Beaubocuf, a student at Philadelphia College of Osteopathic Medicine, watch on a Jumobotron as Pope Francis moves among the pilgrims.
*Jonathan Wilson / For The Inquirer*

**ABOVE RIGHT:** People climbed a tree to gain a better vantage to see and take photos of Pope Francis during his parade around the Ben Franklin Parkway. *Clem Murray / Staff Photographer*

**BELOW RIGHT:** Pilgrims cheer and wave as Pope Francis drives up the Parkway to Mass. *Matthew Hall / For The Inquirer*

**OPPOSITE:** Pope Francis arrives for the papal Mass on the Parkway. *David Maialetti / Staff Photographer*

**OPPOSITE:** The pope's altar on the Parkway. *David Maialetti / Staff Photographer*

**LEFT:** Danielle Orellana lifts her hands in prayer at the papal Mass on the Parkway. *David Swanson / Staff Photographer*

**BELOW LEFT:** Elizabeth Mahon (right), Allison George (center), and Larissa Abaidoo (left) are all attention during Pope Francis' Mass on the Parkway. *Elizabeth Robertson / Staff Photographer*

**BELOW RIGHT:** Francisca Javier, left, and Meriam Peralta, third from right, look up at a Jumbotron as the pope celebrates Mass. *Jonathan Wilson / For The Inquirer*

**ABOVE:** Pennsylvania Gov. Tom Wolf (far right) and his wife, Frances, attend the Papal Mass on the Benjamin Franklin Parkway with Joseph Neubauer and his wife, Jeaneatte (third from left). *Michael Bryant / Staff Photographer*

**LEFT:** Eastern Rite Catholic bishops put their crown-like miters on the chairs behind them as they concelebrate Mass with Pope Francis. *Michael Bryant / Staff Photographer*

**OPPOSITE:** Cantor Charlene Angelini leads worshippers in song at the papal Mass on the Parkway.

*Jessica Griffin / Staff Photographer*

**RIGHT:** Pope Francis walks onto the stage in the procession for the start of Mass on the Parkway.

*Michael Bryant / Staff Photographer*

**OPPOSITE:** A panoramic view of the hundreds of thousands of pilgrims who gathered to worship with Pope Francis.

*Matt Slocum / Associated Press*

**ABOVE:** Pope Francis preaches on the Parkway. *Michael Bryant / Staff Photographer*

**RIGHT:** Hands folded in prayer, a woman fixes her gaze on a Jumbotron at Love Park during Mass. *Charles Fox / Staff Photographer*

**FAR RIGHT:** Another woman watches the pope on the Love Park Jumbotron. *Charles Fox / Staff Photographer*

**OPPOSITE:** The pope raises the consecrated host at Mass as Archbishop Chaput looks on. *Michael Bryant / Staff Photographer*

**ABOVE:** The Rev. Francis Xavier gives communion to Victoria Sylvanus, a homeless woman from Port Richmond. *David Swanson / Staff Photographer*

**RIGHT:** At a Mass unlike any other, security fences become communion rails.

*Bradley C. Bower / For The Inquirer*

**ABOVE:** Pilgrims struggled to the front of the crowd to receive communion during the Parkway Mass. *Elizabeth Robertson / Staff Photographer*

**ABOVE:** Pope Francis leans over to bless a child who helped bring up the bread and wine to be consecrated at Mass. *Michael Bryant / Staff Photographer*

**ABOVE:** Pope Francis arrives at Philadelphia
International Airport for his return flight to Rome
on Sept. 27. *Steven M. Falk / Staff Photographer*

# CHAPTER SIX

# FAMILY & FAITH

T he World Meeting of Families, the great Vatican convocation that drew Pope Francis to Philadelphia, was meant to explore the ways that family shapes individuals and societies and the cultural forces that threaten family life.

In advance of the international gathering, convened by the Catholic Church but open to people of all faiths, The Philadelphia Inquirer took a look at the ways family functions in the 21st century. Powerful forces tear at family life: death, disease, poverty, hunger, violence, disability. Yet families cope, with their faith and the help of their church.

Here, from Africa to Philadelphia to Texas, are stories of faith and family, the two forces at the heart of the World Meeting of Families.

---

**OPPOSITE:** Jillian Nguyen, 3, the daughter of immigrants from Vietnam, peeks around during a baptism ceremony at St. Helena Catholic Church in Philadelphia. Jillian was baptized along with her parents, Stanley Nguyen and Thuong Dinh, and her sister, Lillian, 10. *Elizabeth Robertson / Staff Photographer*

# In Kenya, a church that serves all

By David O' Reilly | Inquirer staff writer

**M**ALINDI, Kenya — In this desperately poor city on Africa's east coast, where jobs are few, HIV is rife, and child care is left mostly to women, few families match the happy ideal held forth by the World Meeting of Families that took place in Philadelphia in 2015.

Just one household in five has two parents raising the children and able to make ends meet. "It's a mess," says the Rev. Albert Buijs, vicar for the Roman Catholic Diocese of Malindi.

Yet thanks to international relief organizations and a diocesan network of 17 parishes, 33 priests, 63 nuns and six brothers, the Roman Catholic presence in Malindi provides a breadth of operation that no single mosque or Christian congregation here can match.

"We are here for the service of all," says Bishop Emanuel Barbara, a 66-year-old missionary of the Capuchin Franciscan order, to which Philadelphia Archbishop Charles J. Chaput belongs.

Only 40,000 of the half million people who live within the Diocese of Malindi are Catholic. About half the population is Muslim; the rest are Christian or belong to traditional animist faiths.

"We don't distinguish between Catholics and Christians and Muslims," says Barbara. "For us, the human person comes first. But mostly, we target the poor."

Such compassion helps explain why Catholicism is growing faster in Africa — where the church cares for about half of all with AIDS and HIV — than on any other continent. Two hundred million Africans are Catholic — 16 percent of the church's membership worldwide.

Founded in 2000, the modest Malindi diocese operates a network of 36 primary and 19 secondary schools, where 40 percent of pupils are Muslim.

It runs five health clinics; promotes clean water projects; teaches agriculture, animal husbandry and hygiene; makes microfinance loans; operates a spacious, cheerful shelter for sexually abused children; runs outreach to prostitutes seeking to

**LEFT:** Evelyn Akinya fries fish in a shack in the very poor coastal city of Malindi to sell to passersby. She also supports her three children by washing neighbors' clothes. Akinya, who struggles with HIV, finds hope in Catholicism, as do 200 million others in Africa.

*For The Philadelphia Inquirer / Georgina Goodwin*

**OPPOSITE:** Under a painting of the Holy Family, parishioners worship at St. Francis Xavier in Malindi on Kenya's north coast.

*For The Philadelphia Inquirer / Georgina Goodwin*

## If I live in this house, there is no hope for the future.

EVELYN AKINYA

quit; and maintains two homes for disabled children.

It also tends to people of all faiths struggling with HIV or AIDS, like 22-year-old washerwoman Evelyn Akinya..

Carrying her infant daughter with her two older children in tow, she leads two diocesan health-care workers down the twisting alleys of a shantytown to a 7- by 9-foot storeroom in her aunt's cinderblock house.

On the floor are two thin foam pads, the mattresses where Kevin, 11, Jacquelin, 4, and Douline, 1, sleep with their mother.

This room is their home.

Sister Margaret Obwoge and Rhoda Nyambwogi sit to hear her story.

Hungry for affection, she was seduced by a 20-year-old man and gave birth to Kevin when she was 11. The man soon abandoned them.

She was married at 17 to a man who drank heavily and beat her. He also sired her two other children and was the source of her and Jacquelin's HIV, which the girl contracted in utero.

Akinya fled her abusive marriage after four years and moved into this storeroom in her aunt's home. "But I am not welcome," she says in a soft voice. "If I live in this house, there is no hope for the future."

When Akinya a Catholic, mentions

that none of her children was baptized, Sister Margaret replies, "I will see to it." And when she speaks of having a "chest problem," Nyambwogi says she will have her tested for tuberculosis — a significant health problem for HIV patients in Kenya's slums.

Outside, both health workers are distraught. "This is among the worst I've ever seen," Sister Margaret says, and the two begin identifying the steps they need to take.

"Beds would cost 35,000 shillings," or about $38, says Sister Margaret, and getting the family into a new home might cost $100. Nyambwogi agrees. "We have to get them out of there," she says.

For all its grinding poverty, Malindi is a paradise — for foreigners. Its oceanfront became a popular resort destination for Europeans, especially Italians, starting in the 1960s.

The flow of wealthy tourists "has been a mixed blessing," says Buijs, a Dutch-born missionary (pronounced bowse) who also serves as a parish pastor. Now 74, he has ministered in Kenya for 45 years.

"Tourism gives the people jobs," he says. "But it has also brought with it prostitution, child abuse, human trafficking, and AIDS."

Nearly a quarter of all girls in the Malindi region between ages 12 and 18 trade sex for money or favors, a 2006 study by UNICEF found, with about half starting by age 14.

And that was when times were good.

Since 2013, the radical Islamist group al-Shabaab, the Somali arm of al-Qaeda, has conducted a string of massacres across Kenya, leaving 67 dead at a shopping mall in Nairobi and 60 Christians slaughtered last June in Mpeketoni, a town at the north end of the Malindi diocese. About half were Catholic.

Then, in April, on Holy Thursday, its soldiers murdered 148 Christian students at a college in Garissa, near the Somali border.

As a result, tourism is draining away, putting thousands out of work and straining already fragile families to the breaking point. Two-thirds of the population already lives below the "absolute poverty" line of 200 Kenyan shillings, or $2, a day.

Sadly, many of the region's most desperate families look to prostitution as "a way to put food on the table," the UNICEF study found. The report estimated that 15,000 women under 18 were engaged in prostitution in Malindi and three other coastal cities.

Barbara, who became Malindi's bishop in 2011, concluded that children fleeing prostitution, incest, unwanted marriage and other abuses needed a safe haven. He vowed that if he could raise the money, he would name the shelter after Pope Francis. And the money came, $2.9 million, from an American real estate developer.

None of Malindi's Catholic clergy expects the bruising poverty here to end soon. Malindians fear that Al-Shabaab's vow to make Kenya's cities "red with blood" has scared off the wealthy foreigners for good.

Civic leaders must cultivate new sources of revenue, Bishop Barbara has told them, but he says, "I see very little happening."

Still, many of his flock take comfort in the belief that a loving God watches over them.

Inside St. Francis Xavier Church, where Buijs is pastor, the 700 seats are filled to overflowing on Sunday mornings.

The elaborate processional features six altar boys in white cassocks, 100 men who have just finished a diocesan retreat, a dozen young girls dancing in T-shirts and white satin skirts, a man carrying a Bible over his head, and three priests.

"Bwana Ulinde," cries the choir in Swahili: "Lord, God."

"Watato wako," the congregation replies: "Save the children."

Later, when another procession brings gifts of flour, beans, sugar, vegetables, bananas, mangoes and bread to the altar, Sister Margaret tells a visitor: "I will be bringing those to families tomorrow."

The collection plate on a typical Sunday brings in about $200 — about 30 cents for each parishioner.

The Mass, in Swahili, lasts three hours and eight minutes. "Why not?" Buijs asks afterward, feigning surprise that anyone would think it lengthy. "It's a celebration."

It's also plenty of time to study the large mural of the Holy Family to the left of the altar. Mary, a black African, is smiling as she weaves a basket. A black Joseph also smiles as he clasps a hand on young Jesus' head.

But Jesus is not smiling. Looking about 6, in shorts and sandals, he is holding a hammer, about to strike the first of three large nails — a clear foreshadowing of his crucifixion. His reproachful glance at Joseph seems to ask: "Do you know what awaits me?"

It is the somber question that seems to hang over all of the Malindi region, especially its young.

*Watato wako.*

# Gift helps church shelter Kenya's poor

By David O' Reilly | Inquirer staff writer

The creation of Pope Francis Home – a transitional home for abused and at-risk children in this very poor coastal city – shines a light on the ways the Catholic Church is present in some of the poorest parts of the world.

It is a presence that includes the priests and nuns and brothers of the diocese, with international relief agencies, Vatican assistance for church construction, and the compassion of lay people in far parts of the globe.

Early last year, Catholic Relief Services (CRS), the Baltimore-based international relief agency of the U.S. Conference of Catholic Bishops, got word that a wealthy American, Brian Soukup, of Fort Collins, Colo., wished to build an orphanage in Africa.

"We didn't know what to say," Lane Bunkers, CRS' officer in Kenya, recalled at his Nairobi office. "We don't do orphanages anymore."

Instead of warehousing parentless children until they turn 18 – the the model of decades past – CRS and most similar organizations now seek to place at-risk children with families, Bunkers said.

"And so we explained to Mr. Soukup our current thinking. Then we told him that the bishop of Malindi had been trying for years to raise money for a transitional shelter for children, and that it was going very slowly. Would he consider doing something different?"

Soukup agreed to fund, at a cost of $2.9 million, the Pope Francis Home according to the vision of the missionary bishop of Malindi, Emanuel Barbara: a home for abused and other vulnerable children.

"My only goal was to help the poorest of the poor," Soukup, 61, explained.

By age 40, he had made a fortune in commercial and residential real estate in Colorado and was able to semi-retire, he said. He now spends much of his time at his ranch, "doing things like irrigation and fixing fences."

A devout Catholic, he was serving on the board of Catholic Charities USA, he said, "when the situation in Malindi came up."

"A lot of people overuse the word *blessed,* but the man upstairs took

**OPPOSITE:** Workmen prepare a concrete ramp for a building at the St. Francis Home. The shelter was built with a $2.9 million gift from Colorado real estate developer Brian Soukup.
*For The Philadelphia Inquirer / Georgina Goodwin*

**LEFT:** Workmen shovel sand at the Pope Francis Home for sexually abused children in Malindi, Kenya. The home will provide a refuge for children for up to five months until they can be placed with families.
*For The Philadelphia Inquirer / Georgina Goodwin*

> A lot of people overuse the word blessed, but the man upstairs took good care of me. So I feel it's my duty to take care of others.
>
> BRIAN SOUKUP

**ABOVE RIGHT:** The Rev. Albert Buijs, Dutch-born pastor of St. Francis Xavier, sprinkles the congregation with holy water.

*For The Philadelphia Inquirer / Georgina Goodwin*

good care of me," he said. "So I feel it's my duty to take care of others."

The complex of buildings spreads over 2 ½ acres. The land, along with a large, thatched-roof home, was donated by an Italian family who used it for a vacation home.

All of the structures are painted cream or yellow inside, their pebbly exteriors gray with lime trim.

The Rev. Bernard Malasi, head of the Malindi Diocese's Office for Children, and construction supervisor Shaba Mweni offered a quick tour to a visitor during the construction.

Built of stuccoed cinder-block, spare yet handsome, each single-story building features a corrugated green roof and concrete floors. The buildings include offices, a convent for four nuns, a dining room and kitchen, separate dormitories for boys and girls, open-air sitting areas, a 10-bed maternity ward, and a wide chapel where purple-and-white conch shells already serve as the holy water fonts.

The trunk of a neem tree, native to the region, stands at the base of the altar. (A few dozen ants still called it home. )

"Most of the children have never seen anything like this in their life," said Mweni. At present, many sexually abused children are sent to shabby state homes with few resources.

Malasi said the home is meant to house girls up to age 18, but only boys 15 and younger. "We don't want unnecessary problems," he explained.

While children of all faiths are welcome, the campus will not have mosques or chapels for other faiths, the bishop said, because they are difficult to administer.

The completion of the home was to be followed by construction of a Catholic primary school nearby to serve the home's residents and outside students, whose tuitions will defray some the home's operating costs.

"We also don't want them hidden away," said the Rev. Albert Buijs, vicar of the diocese, "because there's no reason for them to be ashamed."

**LEFT:** A child strolls the aisle during Mass at St. Francis Xavier.

*For The Philadelphia Inquirer / Georgina Goodwin*

# New Jersey parish a source of solace

By Julia Terruso | Inquirer staff writer

Luis Medina's eyes wandered upward to the stained glass windows of St. Joseph Pro-Cathedral in Camden. He tapped his ring finger against his thumb and swayed in the pew.

Medina, 23, stood beside his much younger peers, who focused their eyes on the bishop who would confirm them.

With very limited language and the cognitive skills of a 4-year-old, Medina, who has autism, is locked in his own world but is every bit a part of St. Joseph's. He finds comfort in the familiar tenor of the cantor's voice, the call and response cadence of the Mass.

"He's an individual, he's a person that needs special supports, but we still want to give him the chance to be able to do everything all the other families do," said his mother, Susana, who prepared him for confirmation. "Whatever he learns, he learns. He may not be able to grasp all of it, but you have to give him that opportunity."

Susana and her husband, Hector, of Camden, have been bringing Luis to St. Joseph's since he was a baby. Both are Eucharistic ministers and parish volunteers. Luis was baptized in this tight-knit place, where everyone holds hands during the Our Father and the exchange of peace lasts five minutes, as parishioners crisscross the church to embrace friends.

Luis needs 24/7 monitoring. Now that he's gotten stronger with age — about 5 feet 6 and 200 pounds — two people have to be around him in public, in case he tries to run away. He can't communicate easily if agitated, which makes bringing him to crowded places difficult.

But the Medinas don't want to keep him inside. They want him in the light of the community and their faith.

So does the Catholic Church. The U.S. Conference of Catholic Bishops has encouraged all parishes to make their facilities accessible and "embrace our responsibility to our own disabled brothers and sisters."

Hector and Susana met taking college courses in Massachusetts and moved to Camden in 1989. They had Hector in 1990 and Luis in 1991. Each also has three children from previous marriages.

When Luis was almost 2, he fell backward in his crib and started seiz-

> ## Whatever he learns, he learns. He may not be able to grasp all of it, but you have to give him that opportunity.
>
> SUSANA MEDINA

ing. Doctors could not immediately diagnose him. Once home from the hospital, his behavior became strange.

"It was like something stopped," Susana said. He'd sit by himself and tap on the four corners of a table. They took him to a specialist at Cooper University Hospital, where he was diagnosed with autism.

In February 2013, tragedy struck the Medinas. Luis got off a bus after

OPPOSITE: Susana Medina and son Luis Medina after his confirmation at St. Joseph Pro-Cathedral in Camden. The church has affirmed that people with disabilities should have access to the sacraments.

*Elizabeth Robertson / Staff Photographer*

a school program, darted away from his aide and banged on a neighbor's door. The homeowner, possibly mistaking them for intruders, opened fire, hitting Luis in a shoulder and the caregiver in the chest. Both survived. The Prosecutor's Office determined there was no criminal conduct involved in the shooting.

"I think our faith got us through it," Susana said. "Being spiritual is the best medicine." She and her husband worry sometimes about what lies ahead — more misunderstandings — or the day when they can no longer care for their son. She tries to suppress those fears by focusing on the next day, the next milestone.

At least 500 members of the community filled St. Joseph for the confirmation. Red and white rose bouquets decorated the altar. Young women wore white dresses. Luis wore a dress shirt and tie, his rosary around his neck.

Afterward, the families filed outside to pose with the bishop. When it was Luis' turn, he yelled "cheese" " as his mother snapped a photo.

Out in the parking lot, he hugged his mother and then his father, who kissed him on the cheek. "You know who I am?" Hector whispered into his son's ear. "Dad," Luis said in a low whisper.

"You're the love of my life," his father whispered back, flicking a tear off his cheek.

# Father's death tests family's faith

By David O' Reilly | Inquirer staff writer

OPPOSITE: The Vesey and Gregor families of Newtown, Bucks County, gather at Kelly Vesey's shore home in Longport. Widow Kelly and widower Mike Gregor will marry next year, creating a blended family. Front row, from left: Kelly, 50; Mike, 52; and Michael Vesey, 10. Middle row, from left: Kelly Gregor, 21 and Shannon Vesey, 18. Back row, from left: Jack Gregor, 19; Caitlyn Vesey, 16; Katy Gregor, 23, and Lauren Vesey, 14.

*Tom Gralish / Staff Photographer*

BELOW: Pope Benedict XVI blesses Mike Vesey and his family before Mass at St. Peter's Basilica as they return from a pilgrimage to Medjugorje in Bosnia-Herzegovina. Vesey died in 2009, but his family's faith remains strong. *Courtesy of Vesey family*

The best of families can be battered and reshaped by forces beyond their control.

When a brain scan revealed that Mike Vesey had brain cancer, he and his family embarked on a twin-track journey of medical science and religious faith that would include surgeries, special Masses, experimental treatments, a pilgrimage, a papal blessing, rosaries prayed on nearly every car ride, moments of triumph, plunging disappointments and many tears.

Four years after his diagnosis, Vesey, president of Orleans Home Builders in Bensalem, died at age 50.

Their shared struggle brought the Vesey family even closer, they say. Yet it left the children mystified about God's ways.

"We went on a pilgrimage to a Third World country," said 14-year-old Lauren as she sat with her siblings around their kitchen counter in Newtown, Bucks County.

"What's the point of doing that if it doesn't help?"

"We prayed for four years," Caitlyn, 16, recalled. "I don't get it. Four years."

Their mother, Kelly, also knows what it's s like to be a teenager feeling baffled, even betrayed by God. She was 18, about to start college, when her father, Dennis Mehigan, dropped dead of a heart attack at age 42.

In addition to Kelly, he left three sons, ages 17, 15, and 9, and a widow who had not worked outside the home since they were married.

The loss was unfathomable. Kelly wanted little to do with the Catholic Church: "I lost my faith."

But in 1992, nine years after her father's death, she met the man who would reconnect her to God and the church she had abandoned. Mike Vesey would restore the faith she drew on as his own life slipped away.

As they began dating, Mike — a devout Catholic — urged Kelly to work out her anger with God and the church. She did, with the help of a priest from her mother's parish, St. Mary's in Cherry Hill.

"There's evil in the world," she recalled the Rev. David Grover telling her. "God cannot control everything. But he is there to love and support us. And he will put people in your life to help you get through."

Soon, Kelly said she was attending Mass "pretty regularly." Four years later, she and Mike were married at St. Andrew's Roman Catholic Church in Newtown.

Kelly, a nurse-practitioner, quit after Lauren's birth in 2002 to be an at-home mom. And when Shannon, now 18, started Catholic kindergarten the next year, Kelly decided to pray the rosary for Lent.

She climbed into bed one night with a new rosary and Mike gave her a look. "Don't tell me you're going to turn into one of those holy rollers," he said. No worries, she assured him.

Neither could imagine that in

two years, she would be his fiercest prayer warrior.

"I really think God was preparing me for what was going to come," she said, "so that this time, I wouldn't turn away."

Believing Mike had just three months to live after his diagnosis, she taught him to pray the rosary, and the two began attending Wednesday night prayer groups.

It seemed to make a difference. Two years after surgery, the tumor had not returned, and so the family decided to give thanks with a pilgrimage to the shrine of Mary in Medjugorje, Bosnia-Herzegovina, and to St. Peter's Basilica in Rome, where Pope Benedict XVI embraced Mike before Mass.

"We thought Mike was being miraculously healed," Kelly recalled But weeks later, a new brain scan revealed that his tumor had begun to grow. "We were devastated," she said.

By year's end, Mike was losing strength on his right side and the ability to speak.

He began using a cane, then a walker, then a wheelchair, and in his final weeks, moved to a spare bedroom, visited or tended round the clock by hospice workers, friends, siblings, his mother, in-laws, his pastor, and his wife and children.

The children baked cookies that read, "I love you, Dad," and made him ceramic plates and cups so fragile that nearly all broke.

Unable to speak in his final days, he nonetheless astonished everyone when he found the voice to recite one Hail Mary as Msgr. Michael Picard, his friend and pastor at St. Andrew's, prayed the rosary over him. It was far from the miracle they had hoped for, but it left Kelly feeling he was "being held by God and the Blessed Mother."

Mike Vesey died Aug. 28, 2009.

Though their fervent prayers did not yield the miracle they hoped for, said Lauren, "it helped us get through" the long ordeal of their father's cancer and death.

"We know Dad is like a second guardian angel, watching over us," she said.

And it seems that the God who sometimes sends rain on the righteous sends sunshine, too.

Two years ago, Kelly met another Mike.

A widower, with children ages 23, 21, and 19, Mike Gregor belongs to St. Andrew's parish. He and Kelly are engaged to be married in 2016.

Seeing their mother with another man "was definitely hard at first," said Shannon.

But after a time, she and her siblings came to realize that a husband in their mother's life "could be a blessing. We looked at the alternatives and realized, Dad's not coming back."

"You know Dad's happy for her," said Lauren. "And happy for us."

# Church closings, illness don't dim faith

By Kristin E. Holmes | Inquirer staff writer

> I was laying on the gurney and thinking, I can't take all of this [worry] with me. I'm letting go of it and turning it over.
>
> CARLA CAPLE

In the Southwest Philadelphia neighborhood where Carla Caple has lived since birth, maintaining a faith life has been like a game of musical chairs.

One Catholic parish closes and Caple moves to another. Then that church shuts down and she goes on to the next.

Since 2010, the archdiocese has reorganized and reduced the number of parishes in the five-county area from 266 to 219. The dizzying changes are part a national trend that started in the Midwest in the 1970s, affecting most major dioceses.

"It seemed like it was just the inner city, but then [the closings] started spreading to the suburbs," Caple said.

Through each closing or merging of a parish and school, Caple has enrolled her children at someplace new and gone to Mass with a new group of congregants.

"The church has always been a part of my life, because I was raised in the church," she said. "I was taught that you can't just call on God in the time of need. You have to constantly do it, and I pray every day."

Now a parishioner at St. Cyprian Church, Caple said her faith has carried her through some dark days.

"The church has helped me in dealing with everything in my life," she said. "It's always been there to help. "

That was especially true when, at 34, the former certified nursing assistant was diagnosed with a torn heart valve and underwent surgery. Weeks later, she suffered a stroke. "There was nothing I could do about it," Caple said of her illnesses. "I turned it over [to God]."

Caple, now 38, shared her experience with fellow parishioners for the first time in April on Good Friday, she said. During a service based on the "Seven Last Words of Christ," phrases that Christians believe Jesus spoke from the cross, Caple talked about the seventh: "Father, into thy hands I commend my spirit" (Luke 23:46).

"You know how you go to church, and you think what they're saying has nothing to do with you? " Caple said. "Well, ... ."

Caple's faith tradition goes back generations. Her mother and grandmother worshipped at St. Rita's in South Philadelphia before moving to Transfiguration of Our Lord parish at 56th Street and Cedar Avenue.

Caple grew up in Transfiguration and attended its school. She went on to middle school at Most Blessed Sacrament at 56th Street and Chester Avenue, then West Catholic High School in 1989, soon after the girls' and boys' schools merged.

Eventually, she began her career as a nursing assistant, supporting a family that grew to include daughter Aliah, now 19, and son Kenneth Washington Jr., 10.

Both youngsters attended Catholic schools, including Our Lady of the Blessed Sacrament parish at 63d and Callowhill Streets, where Caple worshipped before joining St. Cyprian.

In 2011, Caple was at her job in a nursing facility when her chest began to hurt. After two weeks of medical appointments and tests, doctors discovered the tear in Caple's heart valve. She was told she needed surgery immediately.

So serious was her condition that she was advised to complete an advance directive. Her doctor asked for instructions about her choice of a funeral home and her child-custody wishes.

"There was no guarantee that I was going to wake up off that table,"

Caple said.

Her faith sustained her. Just as Jesus on the cross put his fate in the hands of his father, she said, she recited the Lord's Prayer before she was wheeled into the operating room.

Doctors cracked open her chest and repaired the heart valve, but her recovery was complicated. A month later, Caple was at home resting when she suddenly got cold and felt tingling in her right arm, which later went numb.

A nurse coincidentally visiting that day told Caple that she was having — or had had — a stroke.

"We called 911 and the ambulance came," Caple said.

Since then, Caple's life has included a seemingly never-ending series of checkups, tests, and physical therapy.

"I can't walk up the steps without panting, and some days my hands and arms hurt," Caple said. She had to stop working and go on disability.

Then in 2012, Our Lady of the Blessed Sacrament school closed while Kenneth was a student, and the parish closed a year later. Kenneth enrolled at St. Frances Cabrini Regional School, the former St. Donato's, at 65th Street and Callowhill.

"He was heartbroken," Caple said. "He loved that school."

Caple had felt the same when the archdiocese, in 2000, closed Transfiguration, the parish where she grew up. Caple returned to St. Cyprian at Cobbs Creek Parkway and

Cedar, which she had attended after Transfiguration merged with what became St. Cyprian.

"At first I was upset," Caple said, thinking of the church she calls "Transy" and the wave of West and Southwest Philadelphia church closings that followed.

Caple's children ultimately wound up in non-Catholic schools, Kenneth at a public school and Aliah in a cyber high school.

But the Catholic Church remains the family's spiritual home. On Good Friday, when Caple talked from the pulpit about her medical struggles, she said she chose the theme of the seventh word — trust in the face of fear — because it fit her experience, particularly coping with illness.

"I was laying on the gurney and thinking, I can't take all of this [worry] with me," Caple said. "I'm letting go of it and turning it over."

**ABOVE:** Carla Caple with daughter, Aliah Caple, 19, and son, Kenneth Washington Jr., 10, on Cobbs Creek Parkway in Philadelphia. She has moved from parish to parish because of mergers and closings.

*Alejandro A. Alvarez / Staff Photographer*

# Vietnamese family finds faith together

By Kristin E. Holmes | Inquirer staff writer

Stanley Nguyen began attending church as a kind of thank you to people who helped him after he came to the United States as one of the Boat People in the late 1970s.

When the family that offered him a place to live and work went to a Catholic church, Nguyen went, too, but it wasn't until he settled in Philadelphia, nearly 25 years after fleeing war-ravaged South Vietnam, that religion became personal.

In April, Nguyen was baptized at St. Helena Roman Catholic Church in Olney, along with his wife, Thuong Dinh, and two daughters, Lillian, 10, and Jillian, 3. Two weeks later, the family gathered again at the church as Nguyen and his wife were married in a religious ceremony, 13 years after they first said "I do."

At St. Helena's, Nguyen, 56, an office worker for a cleaning company, found a church with a thriving Vietnamese community and a multicultural mix that mirrors its Philadelphia neighborhood.

Parishioners at the 1,200-family congregation are Vietnamese, Latino, African American, African, and white. Msgr. Joseph T. Trinh, who emigrated from Vietnam, leads a diverse staff of clergy. He is also the head of the Philadelphia-based, 1.5-million-member Federation of Vietnamese Catholics, a national group.

"For Vietnamese Catholics, the church is the center of everything, the spiritual and social," Trinh said.

In South Vietnam, Nguyen's only connection to the Catholic Church was through school.

One of seven children, Nguyen attended a Catholic school in Bac Lieu province, where his family owned a small variety store. The family religion was "ancestor worship," Nguyen said, a tradition that venerates dead family members.

Nguyen, whose birth name is Thien, worked at the store seven days a week. In 1970, the family moved to Saigon to open a new store, but when North Vietnamese troops took the city, Nguyen and his family returned to Bac Lieu and became farmworkers.

With the economy crushed by the war and the communists in power, Nguyen said, he decided to leave. "I felt like I had no future," he said.

In 1979, Nguyen boarded a small fishing boat crowded with 100 people and left home, eventually ending up in Indonesia. He spent months in refugee camps before a group of Jaycees from Indiana sponsored him. He landed in Evansville, Ind., and stayed with a Catholic family that worked in construction. Nguyen worked with them and joined them at church. "It brought back memories of school," he said.

Nguyen learned English, earned his GED, and attended college. He moved to Boston, then Las Vegas. He worked as a road surveyor and even tried playing professional poker.

He chose the name Stanley after seeing the movie *"The Year of the Dragon,"* with Mickey Rourke as a police detective and decorated Vietnam veteran named Stanley White.

In 1999, Nguyen moved to Philadelphia, where a brother had settled. He dabbled in business, starting a short-lived Vietnamese TV station. He met Trinh while covering an event for the station. Nguyen found Trinh — called "Holy Trinh-ity" on the church website — to be someone with a similar background and experiences and he began going to Trinh's church regularly.

By then, Nguyen had traveled back to Vietnam and met Dinh. They married in a civil ceremony, but Dinh remained in Vietnam, stuck behind a wall of immigration paperwork. Lillian was born while Nguyen was in the United States.

St. Helena's brought Nguyen solace while he and Dinh were apart. "I felt like I had a big family even though

my wife wasn't here," he said.

In 2007, Dinh and Lillian finally joined him. Five years later, Jillian was born.

Nguyen began taking his daughters to church with him, but his wife, raised a Buddhist, was reluctant to go. "I talked her into it," Nguyen said.

"Lillian was going to [St. Helena's-Incarnation] school, and they were going to church," Dinh, 38, explained in Vietnamese, translated by her husband. " I just wanted the family to be together."

The timing couldn't have been better. "The pope is coming," Nguyen mused not long after the ceremony, "so I guess I got baptized at the right time and place."

**ABOVE:** Stanley Nguyen is baptized by Msgr. Joseph T. Trinh at St. Helena's. Nguyen, whose family practiced ancestor worship, left Vietnam in the late 1970s as one of the Boat People.

*Elizabeth Robertson / Staff Photographer*

# Church offers haven in Houston

By Julia Terruso | Inquirer staff writer

Ana Ulloa Romero and her two younger children reached their arms over the car tire supporting them as they propelled themselves through the murky Rio Grande toward the hope of something better. Debris and water started filling the tire, pulling them downward and scaring the younger ones, whom Romero comforted with quick prayers.

*Please God, protect my family.*

Somewhere in the desert expanse ahead of them, Romero's husband, Oscar, was crossing with "coyotes," human smugglers. She would learn later how the so-called safe house became a torture chamber where the coyotes beat the men and raped the women; how he was often forced to watch, and tried mentally to escape

**LEFT:** In the bedroom that he shares with his parents and a brother in Houston, Franklin Romero, 5, shows a Pre-K excellence award to his father Oscar (middle) and brother Jeffrey, 14. The Romeros, who ran an ice cream shop in their native Honduras, fled gang threats and extortion.

*Elizabeth Robertson / Staff Photographer*

**OPPOSITE:** Hard-pressed to make ends meet, Oscar Romero and his wife Ana Ulloa Romero, both 42, rely on the food pantry at St. Charles Borromeo Parish in Houston to help feed themselves and their three sons.

*Elizabeth Robertson / Staff Photographer*

ABOVE: Jennifer Berlanga Reyes, 8, receives First Communion from the Rev. Christopher Plant at Capilla la Divina Providencia. The chapel draws migrant workers and families in search of a church experience that reminds them of home.

*Elizabeth Robertson / Staff Photographer*

with prayers of his own.

*Please God, let me see my family again.*

One year later, the Romeros are trying to make a life for themselves in Houston. The faith that sustained their journey from Honduras has only strengthened.

For others, like the Reyes family,

the way to the United States has been less perilous but still not easy. Eliseo and Blanca Reyes, fleeing neighborhood gangs in Monterrey, Mexico, simply took their three daughters and one son on a vacation to Houston in 2008 — with no intention of ever returning to Mexico.

Both families are among tens of

thousands of undocumented people who have flocked to the Catholic Church for spiritual and physical support.

Houston is one of the fastest-growing cities in the United States – fueled in large part by its oil and gas industry. It's also one of the most diverse in the nation, a major port of entry for immigrants — legal and illegal — and refugees.

As Catholic churches across the country shutter or consolidate, the Archdiocese of Galveston-Houston faces a different problem – how to provide for its immigrant population, a fearful but faithful group spanning multiple generations and experiences.

"We have so many undocumented, it's incredible, and they live in a certain amount of fear . . .," said Cardinal Daniel DiNardo, the archbishop of Galveston-Houston. The U.S. has "a right to border security, but not at the expense of what's happened to some immigrants," DiNardo added. "They're here to stay. They're not going to leave. Now, we can keep them in the shadows, or we can find better ways to integrate them into who and what we are."

Pope Francis, whose paternal grandparents and their family fled Mussolini's Italy for Argentina in 1928, has called for a change of attitude toward immigrants, "moving away from attitudes of defensiveness and fear, indifference and marginalization — all typical of a throwaway culture — toward attitudes based on a culture of encounter, the only culture capable of building a better, more just, and fraternal world."

New immigrant families, without relatives in the U.S., face immediate concerns of where to go for basic food and shelter.

Ana and Oscar, both 42, and their three sons — ages 16, 14 and 5 — share a $520-a-month, one-bedroom apartment in Magnificat House, a building operated by Catholic nuns primarily to serve people with mental illness. High legal fees have kept the couple from applying for asylum.

When they arrived in Houston after fleeing gang threats and extortion in Honduras in March 2014, the Romeros first moved into an auto shop, where they slept among cars waiting to be repaired.

The Reyes family had a similar experience. Their first home in the U.S. was a garage near the Port of Houston, which cost $430 a month. The owner told them that as undocumented immigrants, they wouldn't qualify for public housing and they couldn't afford anything else.

Catholic Charities has extensive programming for immigrants, starting at the border and continuing into Texas towns and cities with legal aid and housing and health assistance. The organization holds free acculturation sessions, which include English classes, driver's ed, and personal finances.

On a recent Saturday, the Romeros went to the St. Charles Borromeo parish food pantry. A family that was making ends meet in Honduras now is at the mercy of charity and luck to get by. Ana Romero surrenders to frequent tears and unnecessary apologies describing her situation. She says that once her family is situated and her children have grown, she'll encourage them to become missionaries.

Whatever they decide to be, though, this struggle is for them. Franklin, their chatty, bright-eyed 5-year-old and the best English speaker in the family, brought home a certificate for excellence in pre-K. Oscar Jr., 16, is a standout in his school's ROTC program. A photo of him in uniform in front of an American flag is tucked into a box of family mementos.

The Romeros' daughter, Sara, 19, moved to California to ease some of the family's financial burden. She checks in regularly.

Jeffrey, 14, is quiet and thoughtful. At the pantry, he studied a pile of dismantled, computer parts in the corner and started to put the pieces together, one outdated section after the next. He actually got the machine to turn on. His father smiled, impressed at his son's ingenuity.

"I'm happy to see them doing good," Oscar Romero said. "And to continue moving forward."

Like the Romeros, the Reyes family turned to the church for comfort and help. Blanca Reyes started volunteering at Capilla la Divina Providencia, a chapel that draws migrant workers and families in search of a church experience reminiscent of home. For

> They're here to stay. They're not going to leave. Now, we can keep them in the shadows, or we can find better ways than what we're doing to integrate them into who and what we are.
>
> CARDINAL DANIEL DINARDO

Reyes, the church became a social network of support and friendship. She teaches catechism, helping children prepare for First Communion. Her daughter, Jennifer, 8, recently received First Communion at the chapel. Reyes also volunteers at her children's schools, teaches computer classes and enrolled the whole family in an emergency response certification program.

"This country, the church, it's given us the opportunity to be safer," Reyes said. "I can't give money, so I wanted to do what little I can with my hands."

# EPILOGUE

At the end of two jammed and joyous days in Philadelphia, there was a heavy silence punctuated by quiet tears as Pope Francis moved through a select gathering at Philadelphia International Airport to board a flight back to Rome.

Vice President Biden led a delegation to wish Francis well upon his departure.

In brief remarks inside an Atlantic Aviation hangar, Francis said his visit to the United States had been "days of grace for me, and, I pray, for you, too." He reflected on his visit to ground zero in New York City. While he called the site of the terrorist attack a place that speaks of the "mystery of evil," he added, "We know in God's merciful plan, love and peace triumph over all."

The pope said that "this land has been blessed with tremendous gifts and opportunities" and then asked his audience to be "good and generous stewards" of those.

Once again, Francis concluded by requesting that those present pray for him. His last word were: "May God bless you all. God bless America."

**ABOVE:** A final blessing from the pope as he prepares to depart. *Steven M. Falk / Staff Photographer*

Three-year-old Samantha Melso takes cell phone photos of Pope Francis speaking at Independence Hall. *Mary D'Anella / For The Inquirer*

Singing the National Anthem, the faithful gather on Independence Mall to to hear Pope Francis. *David Swanson / Staff Photographer*

# SUPPORTING PARTNERS

# Love. Health. Community.

## WORLD
### MEETING OF
### FAMILIES
2015 Philadelphia

Independence Blue Cross has been enhancing the health and wellness of the people and communities we serve for nearly 80 years. We were proud to help welcome Pope Francis and the World Meeting of Families to Philadelphia for this once-in-a-generation moment.

**Independence** ✚

{

Family life is something worthwhile;
a society grows stronger and better,
it grows in beauty and
it grows in truth, when it rises on
the foundation of the family.

*Pope Francis*

}

We salute The World Meeting of Families for convening a singular event, rich in content
and of lasting impact. Philadelphians will always treasure the special feelings of peace,
friendship and brotherhood inspired by Pope Francis.

The Holy Father demonstrates that when it comes to even intractable problems, it helps
to focus on what we share in common, as precedent to reconciling differences.

We thank Pope Francis for his blessings and for his world leadership.

NEUBAUER FAMILY FOUNDATION

# Honored
to welcome Pope Francis

# Proud
to support our community
and first responders

# Grateful
to our dedicated volunteers

**Wawa®**

# M | Maguire Foundation

**The Maguire Foundation was privileged to be a sponsor of the World Meeting of Families and to have welcomed Pope Francis to Philadelphia during his historic visit.**

Our *mission* is grounded in the teachings of St. Ignatius Loyola that we are men and women for others. The Maguire Foundation's flagship program, The Maguire Scholars' Program, is executed by partnering with educational institutions to provide families of need with scholarship assistance and grants to grade school, high school, and college, building a strong foundation for success.

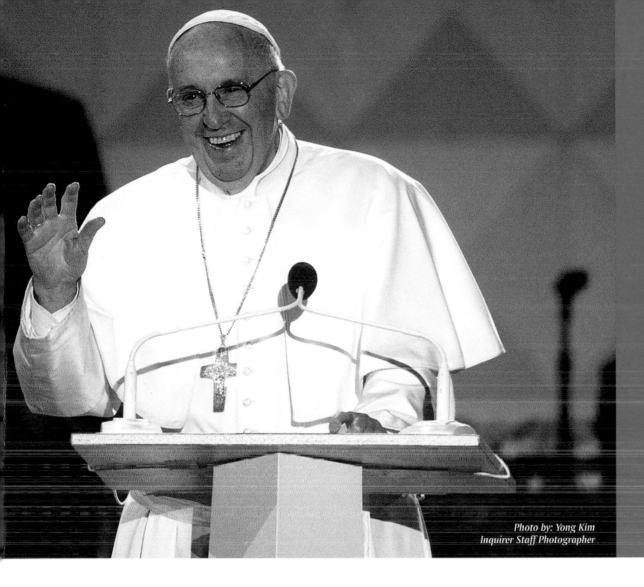

*How proud and fortunate we are to have participated in the remarkable September week of Pope Francis' visit to Philadelphia. And what an inspiring leader he is . . . with compelling words and a gentle smile that charmed local citizens and visitors from afar.*

Photo by: Yong Kim
Inquirer Staff Photographer

# Connelly Foundation

*The weather was glorious as well as the enthusiasm of the diverse crowds, some wearing ethnic dress and speaking in a plethora of languages. A spirit of solidarity extended from river to river in our fair city.*

*We congratulate Archbishop Charles J. Chaput, Mayor Michael A. Nutter, the World Meeting of Families, and the civic leaders and selfless volunteers who planned and orchestrated these unforgettable events.*

*The speech on religious freedom at Independence Hall and the Mass at Eakins Oval will be remembered as gatherings of good-will and become iconic Philadelphia memories, and the Francis Fund will continue the Holy Father's fervent request for charity for the needy.*

# The Nicoletti Family
*proudly supports the*

## 2015 World Meeting of Families